"John Leonard's *Get Real: Sharing Your Ev*  ful read from a man who obviously delights backgrounds, and rejoices in creatively and news of grace in Christ Jesus as 'normally friend. Better yet, he teaches us how to do the same."

Bryan Chapell, Pastor, Grace Presbyterian Church, Illinois; author of *Christ-Centered Preaching*

"Do you know why 'party evangelism' is more biblical than 'friendship evangelism'? Do you know why (and how) to 'evangelize Christians and disciple non-Christians'? Would you like a book about evangelism that is both solidly scriptural and thoroughly practical—and absolutely enjoyable to read? Then *Get Real* by John Leonard is the book for you. No question, this is one of the best books ever on evangelism."

Dr. Samuel Logan, International Director, The World Reformed Fellowship

"When is the last time you talked to someone about Jesus? What comes to mind as you think about that question? Guilt? Frustration? Read John Leonard's *Get Real* to encourage you to think differently about the people and opportunities Jesus brings into your life. Hear great stories from John's experience reaching out to Muslims in France and as a church planter in Philadelphia. Read this book if you want to fall in love with the grace and power of the gospel all over again."

Dr. Tim Witmer, Professor of Practical Theology, Westminster Theological Seminary, Philadelphia; author of *The Shepherd Leader*

"It's always puzzled me how Christians who believe totally in the true humanity of Jesus should use such dehumanized methods to introduce him to others. Thankfully, Leonard has written this excellent book that takes the real Jesus as guide and example to liberate us from all those techniques, and to excite and motivate us to be truly 'personal' in our evangelism. Every evangelist—every Christian—needs to read it."

Dr. John D. Nicholls, Former Chief Executive and Director of Training, London City Mission

"This is simply *the* best book on personal outreach I have ever seen. John Leonard has written for the evangelistically ungifted. Especially beginning in chapter 4, I sensed, 'This material is going to change me.' And it has."

Steven Estes, Pastor; author of *A Better December*; co-author of *When God Weeps*

"This is a disturbing book. In all the right ways. John Leonard brings his considerable wealth of personal experience, cultural awareness, and biblical savvy to this eminently practical guide. Evangelism in Leonard's approach is less daunting, less frightening, and less awkward than it needs to be. What is disturbing is that we can no longer hide behind either bombastic boilerplates or timid excuses. What is comforting is that it allows Christ to do all the heavy lifting. If you are looking for the best resource for training in outreach, both personal and corporate, look no further."

William Edgar, Professor of Apologetics, Westminster Theological Seminary, Philadelphia; author of *Truth in All Its Glory*

"If evangelism seems difficult, or if you have ever said, 'I don't have the gift of evangelism,' you will wish you had read this book a long time ago. The *Get Real* paradigm is anchored in the Scriptures, and especially in the Gospel accounts of Jesus's own process of evangelism. *Get Real* explains in easy-to-understand-and-apply ways that evangelism can be a natural part of a Christian's daily routine. *Get Real* is the material we use to train our missionaries at Mission to the World, and it is appreciated by the missionaries because it works."

Paul Kooistra, Coordinator, Mission to the World

"If you have one book on evangelism in your library, it should be this one. It's not what you expect. It's about life, relationships, and godly inefficiency—and it's about a God who loves us so much that it shows. This is "real deal" evangelism that breaks the rules and opens a floodgate of love and mercy to a desperate and needy world. Reading Dr. Leonard's book is like a drink of cold, clear water refreshing a thirsty soul . . . ours and theirs."

Steve Brown, Key Life radio program Bible teacher; professor, Reformed Seminary; author of *Three Free Sins: God's Not Mad at You.*

"John is a gifted evangelist, which could be intimidating as we watch him in action, but, somehow, he immediately inspired me. As I was reading I got excited about all kinds of conversations up ahead. Being real, listening, and always looking for opportunities for a party—I can do that."

Edward T. Welch, PhD, CCEF Faculty; psychologist; best-selling author

"Like most in the church, I believe in evangelism but am honestly reserved about (afraid of?) practicing it with strangers. (Does teaching and caring for a Sunday school class weekly count as evangelism? I sure hope so!) John Leonard passionately believes in, practices, and teaches many creative ways of doing evangelism. If the world is as desperately in need as our Scripture instructs us it is, then John Leonard's challenging book can teach us bravery. Taste and see!"

Fredrick Dale Bruner, Professor Emeritus, Whitworth University; author of commentaries on Matthew, John, and the Holy Spirit in Acts

"Grace-driven evangelism as a lifestyle versus guilt-driven evangelism as a structured event. John Leonard helps us understand how to be 'real' and 'natural' and 'normal' in sharing the grace and gospel of Christ with others. Jesus loved people and openly shared his life with them as he met them in everyday life. We should do the same, and this book will help you do so more naturally and effectively."

Robert C. (Ric) Cannada Jr., Chancellor Emeritus, Reformed Theological Seminary

Get Real

SHARING YOUR EVERYDAY FAITH EVERY DAY

JOHN S. LEONARD

New
Growth
Press

www.newgrowthpress.com

New Growth Press, Greensboro, NC 27404
www.newgrowthpress.com
Copyright © 2013 by John S. Leonard

Unless otherwise indicated, Scripture quotations are taken from *The Holy
Bible, English Standard Version.* Copyright © 2000, 2001 by Crossway
Bibles, a division of Good News Publishers. Used by permission. All rights
reserved.
   Scripture quotations marked (NIV) are taken from the *Holy Bible,* New
International Version®, NIV®. Copyright © 1973, 1978, 1984, 2011 by Biblica,
Inc. Used by permission. All rights reserved worldwide.
   Scripture quotations marked (NRSV) are taken from the New Revised
Standard Version Bible, copyright © 1989 the Division of Christian
Education of the National Council of the Churches of Christ in the United
States of America. Used by permission. All rights reserved.

Cover Design: Faceout books, faceout.com
Typesetting: Lisa Parnell, lparnell.com

ISBN 978-1-939946-23-2 (Print)
ISBN 978-1-939946-24-9 (eBook)

Library of Congress Cataloging-in-Publication Data
Brooks-Leonard, John, 1955–
   Get real : sharing your everyday faith every day / John S. Leonard. — First
[edition].
      pages cm
   Includes bibliographical references and index.
   ISBN 978-1-939946-23-2 (alk. paper)
   1. Witness bearing (Christianity) I. Title.
   BV4520.B665 2013
   248'.5—dc23   2013024385

Printed in the United States of America

23 22 21 20 19 18 17 16   3 4 5 6 7

Contents

Conclusion

Acknowledgments

I wish I could tell you that everything in this book is mine, but it was modeled by some very important people in my life. I am mostly just telling you what I've learned from them.

The first of those people is Pat Hunter, a lover of God and a lover of people, who understood grace and shared it naturally with others. She touched everyone in her presence. She was a saint. My favorite quote of hers was one of the last words that she spoke to me. She said, "I've known Jesus for seventy years. I ain't got no better; Jesus has only gotten sweeter."

In 1978, I lived and worked as an intern with Dr. William T. Iverson and his family in Newark, New Jersey. I have never met anyone who could naturally turn a conversation to the gospel and illustrate its truths so powerfully.

Most importantly, my wife Christy loves others deeply. She loves because she knows she is wholly and completely loved by the Lord. Christy has shown me the love of Christ and models how I should demonstrate Christ's love.

I would also like to acknowledge our three daughters: Kimberly, Katie, and Betsy whom we love dearly and are so proud of. (Read the conclusion to understand this remark.)

The Gospel We Share

1

Two Ways to Witness

"Hi, my name is Bill. Do you mind if I ask you a few questions?" Without waiting for me to reply, he continued—violating my personal space in an aggressive stance that made me feel threatened. Bill jumped right into his presentation of the gospel. It was one that I knew well.

Bill and his team had come to help us with an outreach, and I had come down early to the auditorium to help set up. Bill had not asked me my name, and in fact didn't seem to want to know anything about me. He just cornered me and "shared." The more he spoke, the more perturbed I became. I felt insulted by the impersonal and dehumanizing way I had been approached. And since Bill had assumed I wasn't a Christian, I decided I would play along, giving him arguments for every point he was trying to make. The more unraveled and frustrated Bill became, the more I enjoyed our conversation.

The sales pitch ended quickly when a mutual friend came up to us and said, "John, I see you've met Bill. Bill, this is John; he is part of our local team and is here to help us with the outreach." Bill's mouth dropped open, looking confused. He stammered, "But . . . are you . . . ? I don't understand. Your answers weren't . . ."

The outreach event went off without a hitch . . . so to speak. It was the typical Christian evangelistic meeting. A room full of Christians filled in as props, listening to other Christians tell them about the gospel, while everyone hoped someone in the room would be saved. But no one came forward when the invitation was given, and given, and given.

After the meeting, Bill came over, looking at me judgmentally. He said, "I still think there is something not quite right." Funny, I was feeling exactly the same way about Bill—but for completely opposite reasons!

❧

Fred rolled into the cafeteria on his three-wheeled scooter. He paused a distance from the table where my wife and I were eating lunch and asked, "May I join you?"

"Sure!" we responded. Everything about Fred communicated safety and acceptance. He was the most nonthreatening person I believe I have ever met.

At the time I was living in the inner city of Detroit with my wife Christy and our two small girls, doing cross-cultural training during the summer, in preparation to go to the mission field that fall. It had been a long, pressure-filled couple of months in the city. We couldn't understand what living in the inner city of Detroit would teach us about life in the south of France, the mission field where we were headed.

I can't tell you anything about Fred, as he never spoke about himself; his only interest was in us. He began asking questions as we shared our lunch together. His questions weren't prying, inappropriate, or just making chit-chat, but invited us into a conversation. Fred was genuinely interested in us. You could see it in his eyes, the tone of his voice, and his body language. He wanted to know us—and we wanted to be known by him!

I can't explain what happened, but as we spoke together, a healing came over us. It felt as if warm oil was being poured over our heads. We could feel it going through our bodies, deep down into our bones, lifting the weight and pressure off of our shoulders, bringing calm over us.

I don't often think of the first encounter with Bill. In fact, I hope I never see Bill again. But Fred, yes—I would love to meet him again.

One reason that we're so reluctant to evangelize is because we believe that evangelism is doing what Bill did—imposing ourselves on others and leaving people cowering, feeling unimportant, used, and violated. We equate evangelism with selling. We see ourselves like those annoying phone solicitors who always seem to call us when we're sitting down to dinner! For this reason many of us run from anything that resembles evangelism. To have the gift of evangelism, it seems, you either need to have the personality of a used-car salesman or the capability to lead someone to Christ while in the 10-items-or-less lane at your local supermarket. If this is what you believe evangelism requires, I can't blame you for not wanting to evangelize.

As Christians, we know we should share our faith with others. However, we don't do it until we feel horribly guilty—then we force ourselves upon some poor, unsuspecting soul. We share the gospel the way they feed geese in France to make *foie gras*. They shove a funnel down a goose's throat and pour in the grain. Likewise, by force-feeding the gospel to others, the outcome of our "sharing" is that our guilt is assuaged. Who cares about the results? We didn't really expect anyone's life to be changed anyway.

The sad reality is that if you've ever watched a movie with caricatures of Christians, the truth is worse than fiction. Evangelism shouldn't be this way.

Evangelism doesn't have to be like my encounter with Bill; it can and should be like the time I spent with Fred. That kind of interaction leaves a deep personal impact. And yet the last word that would come to mind when you consider our interaction with Fred is "evangelism."

We would call what Fred does "counseling." But it has everything to do with evangelism because we were made by God to have deep relationships with him and with others.

Sharing your faith doesn't impose itself on others, leaving them feeling resentful and used. It invites people to step beyond a superficial friendship where no one really cares about listening, and to head toward deep spiritual relationship. It's an approach that makes it safe for people to confide in you and trust you with the truth of what's going on in their lives, so that your interaction with them becomes like warm oil, bringing healing, peace, and grace, lifting the burdens off their shoulders.

A real approach is not a presentation that you memorize, because the gospel you share is shaped by the person the Lord has brought into your life. It is molded by that person's particular circumstances, problems, and struggles. In this approach to evangelism, the gospel is not a one-size-fits-all spandex sweatsuit; it is tailor-made, fitting only one person—the one standing in front of you.

Just because there isn't an outline to memorize doesn't mean this way of sharing your faith is easy. It requires you to have a wide and growing knowledge of the Bible and of our Lord's teachings. One of the best ways to prepare to share your faith is to take notes in Bible study and church—not just to read the Bible, but to study it and absorb it. Read widely so you can be like the scribes of the kingdom our Lord speaks about when he says, "Therefore every scribe who has been trained for the kingdom of heaven is like a master of a house, who brings out of his treasure what is new and what is old" (Matthew 13:52).

At the same time, don't be intimidated if you're a new Christian. New Christians can make the best evangelists. Don't believe for one moment that you don't know enough. You're looking for the people God is leading to himself through you. Therefore, God is going to use you in their lives because you have unique insights and experiences into the gospel that perfectly fit the people you're sharing your faith with.

This book is divided into two parts. The first part is a look at the gospel from Scripture. My prayer is that you will fall in love again in the retelling of the story of the grace of God that is yours in Christ.

Once, when my wife and I were in a difficult place in our marriage, another couple invited us to dinner, unaware of what was going on in our lives. They asked us to share the story of how we met and fell in love. As we retold the story my wife and I fell in love all over again. I hope that you too will fall in love again with the gospel as the story is retold.

The second part of this book is about the way you set the gospel free in your life, so that your interactions with people become sources of grace and healing. Most of the ways we do this are counterintuitive to conventional wisdom.

This book is about grace, not guilt. This book does not guilt you into sharing your faith because you can't share grace if you're under guilt. It's about setting you free so that you'll be able, by God's grace, to impact those around you for Christ.

Discussion Questions

1. How would your feelings about evangelism change if you thought of it more as a "Fred experience" than a "Bill experience"?

2. How can you shift from sharing your faith out of guilt or obligation to sharing as a response to God's grace?

3. What questions do you have about this approach that you hope will be answered in this study?

2

Grace from Beginning to End

I am fascinated by flight, particularly by man's first attempts to get off the ground. I love watching old footage of the things people invented, hoping the contraptions would fly. Perhaps you've seen some of these old films too. For example, there is the "part plane/part umbrella" that begins rattling and shaking on the runway, bouncing off the ground, and then all of a sudden the umbrella breaks in half and falls to the ground. Or the plane that has four layers of wings: as it accelerates, attempting to take off, the wings collapse and the experiment is over.

The most ridiculous footage I know of features a man who has strapped on wooden wings and a tail, and is now standing on a cliff. He begins to flap his wings, and then he jumps off the cliff. The next picture you see is the wooden wings and tail lying on the rocks below. It must be staged because who would do something so stupid? Why would you begin on a *cliff*? If I were him, I would have started on a tree stump. If that didn't work, then I would have tried the front porch, then the barn loft, and maybe the roof. If none of those worked, I would have given up (or broken something) before I ever got to the cliff. Maybe that's exactly what our barnstormer did. If so, he must have convinced himself that if he only had more time and a greater distance from the ground, he could fly. He just needed to try harder.

Our inventor's unrelenting attitude is not that unusual; it isn't stupidity, but stubbornness. The attitude is not "I can do it" but "I *will* do it." We apply this attitude to everything—particularly our relationship with God.

Everyone, in their heart of hearts, believes that if they just have enough time and try hard enough, they can get their relationship with God right. Because this belief is embedded within us, the most difficult part of the gospel for us to accept is grace. Even those of us who say we live by grace look more like the man with the wooden wings and tail and his let's-try-harder mentality.

The person in Scripture who epitomizes the let's-try-harder approach to God is the rich man in Luke 18, who came to Jesus and asked, "Good Teacher, what must I do to inherit eternal life?" (v. 18). The rich man's words confirm what we all know instinctively—something is wrong; something is missing in our lives. The rich man expresses this problem correctly as spiritual in nature. We all desire to know God and to have eternal life, even if we express that need in a nonreligious way.

However, even though the rich man rightly diagnoses his condition, he seeks the wrong cure. He believes that *he* can do it. He asks, "What must *I* do to inherit eternal life?" In these words we see the universal desire for the restoration of our relationship with our Creator, but also the universal belief that if this relationship is going to be restored, it all depends on us. "What must I do, Jesus? Certainly there must be something that I must do, or become, so that God will accept me. Could you please tell me what that *is*?"

This is what makes grace so difficult to accept. We are confident that we have to do it, and in fact would *rather* do it ourselves. It's as if we're saying to God, "I don't need any grace; I can do it. Just tell me what I need to do." Even if we believe we're saved by grace, so ingrained is the idea that "I must do it" that at some point in the process we take over. It is a half-grace thing. Jesus started the work, and it is up to each one of us to finish it. But our salvation, from beginning to end, is the work of God's grace and not our work. If you are going to effectively share the gospel of grace, you must know his grace for yourself.

The rich man not only came with the right question, he came to the right person. He came to Jesus. In the Gospel of John, when the crowds are leaving because of some difficult teaching Jesus had just given, Jesus asks the twelve disciples, "Do you want to go away as well?" Peter answers, "Lord, to whom shall we go? You have the words of eternal life" (John 6:67–68).

But now notice in Luke 18:19 the response of Jesus, "Why do you call me good? There is no one good except God alone." Jesus's words to the rich man are upsetting to many people, but those people are upset for the wrong reasons. They are concerned that Jesus doesn't know who he is. Is Jesus suffering from an identity crisis? We tend to paraphrase his words something like, "Why do you call me good, because only God is good? I'm not quite sure who I am; can you help me?"

However, Jesus is telling the rich man something about himself, something the rich man doesn't want to hear. None of us wants to hear Jesus's words as saying something about *us*. What Jesus says—and what we don't want to believe—is, "No one is good but God alone." Or, more personally, "I am not good," or even more pointedly, "I am evil." The rich man, like most of us, asks a question but doesn't listen to the answer. It blows right by him.

Deaf to the first words that Jesus spoke, the rich man nonetheless hears Jesus mention keeping the Law and responds, "All these I have kept from my youth" (Luke 18:21). In Jewish tradition, before a young man is bar mitzvahed, he is not responsible for what he does. The rich man is informing Jesus that he was keeping the law before the law was required of him; therefore, he should have built up extra credit.

Jesus answers him, "There's just one thing left." The rich man must have become excited. "Yes! Just one last thing and I can have eternal life; just one more thing that I must do."

Jesus tells him, "Sell all that you have and distribute to the poor, and you will have treasure in heaven; and come, follow me" (Luke 18:22). The smile of confidence the rich man must have had a moment earlier immediately became despair and dread because he was absolutely helpless and he knew it.

Jesus, with his response to the rich man, gave him a way to understand his position before God—which this man was completely oblivious to. It's as if Jesus was giving the rich man an altimeter. Let me explain.

I have never skydived, but I'm told that once you've jumped out of the plane, you reach maximum velocity in about twelve seconds. Instead of having a sensation that you are falling, you feel that you are floating in midair. Your sensory perception is being deceived because you have no way of measuring your altitude. Looking at the ground doesn't help because the farmland below looks like a patchwork quilt. If you were to close your eyes you'd think you were floating and could stay that way forever, but just about that time you'd hit the ground at 120 miles an hour.

The rich man didn't want to hear what Jesus was saying to him. He wanted to believe he strapped on his wooden wings and tail and was doing a pretty good job keeping afloat. He couldn't hear Jesus say— "You're not flying; you're falling uncontrollably to your death." We don't want to believe it either.

In the movie *Toy Story*, Woody and Buzz argue about whether he is a real spaceman and whether or not he can fly. Buzz then proves that he can, actually "fly." He bounces off the bed with the shout "To infinity, and beyond!" and through a series of bizarre circumstances, he ricochets off a ball, rebounds into the air, gets slung around in the fan, and lands safely on the bed. All the toys shout, "He flew! He flew!" Exasperatedly, Woody declares, "That wasn't flying; that was falling with style."

Jesus told the rich man and all of us that when it comes to our relationship with God, even the best of us are only falling with style. We are hopelessly and helplessly crashing to the ground, and there is nothing in us that can change our circumstances.

The rich man, like our barnstormer flailing away with his wooden wings and tail, believed he was flying. Jesus's words made him realize he had no hope at all. He wasn't flying; he was falling.

The idea that we must do something to contribute to our salvation, or at least activate it, causes many people to turn Jesus's words into a let's-try-harder approach to Christianity. We, like the rich man, can't hear what Jesus is saying. We interpret Jesus's words—"it is easier for a camel to go through the eye of a needle than for a rich person to enter the kingdom of God" (Matthew 19:24)—not as words of impossibility, but as an exhortation to try harder.

We've even built a theological explanation to support this let's-try-harder interpretation. It has been suggested that Jesus is not talking about a sewing needle but a gate in Jerusalem (gates in the Middle East do resemble a needle's eye). The gate, called Eye of the Needle, is smaller than the main gate. When the main gate is closed, travelers must use the smaller gate. In order for camels to pass through this gate they must have their cargo removed from their backs and get down on their knees. Therefore, the application for this passage becomes "let's try harder!" However, to date, archaeologists have not found such a gate.

Another variation of the let's-try-harder interpretation is to look at the Aramaic words behind our Greek translation of Jesus's statement. In Aramaic, the word for *rope* and *camel* are the same. This interpretation makes Jesus's words literal, a real needle and a real thread, and we all know how difficult it is to get thread through that tiny hole that we can barely see. But *we* can still do it.

Both interpretations try to jump through all kinds of hoops (or a needle's eye), rather than give up on our let's-try-harder approach. They want to hold on to the idea that it is up to us to make things right between God and us. In fact, the harder we make the process on ourselves, the better we like it.

What if the rich man *had* responded to Jesus's words by selling all that he had to gain the kingdom of heaven? What would have been his motivation behind that act? Wouldn't it have been selfishness? Wouldn't it have been the desire to obtain something for him, something that he wanted very much? Is that good?

Paul doesn't think so. In 1 Corinthians 13, he writes, "If I give away all I have, and if I deliver up my body to be burned, but have not love, I gain *nothing*" (1 Corinthians 13:3, emphasis mine). Even if the rich man had said, "All right, Jesus, I'm going to do that to earn my way to heaven," it would not have been enough because the act would have been one of selfishness—not out of love for God, and certainly not out of love for his neighbor.

There is an even more certain way that we know Jesus is not teaching a let's-try-harder approach, but rather showing us that we are falling hopelessly to the ground and not flying. Look at the conversation Jesus has with his disciples immediately afterward. From the people's response to Jesus's conversation with the rich man—"Then who can be saved?" (Luke 18:26)—it is clear that they took Jesus's words to be a literal camel going through a literal needle.

The people are concerned because it is no longer a question about a rich man, but every man. They are thinking, "If you're asking that of a rich man, then what hope can regular people have?"

In the Old Testament, riches were considered a symbol of God's blessings. A rich man was a man who was blessed by God, a man who was close to God, and his wealth was proof that God favored him. If this rich man couldn't get into heaven because of all he had done—and there is no reason to doubt his devotion—what were the chances of regular people gaining eternal life? If you had little, it was already assumed that God cared little for you.

Jesus answered, "What is impossible with men is possible with God" (Luke 18:27). We must hear and understand what Jesus is saying. Jesus teaches that eternal life is something that God must provide because it is beyond anything any of us are capable of obtaining. It's like flying: we can't; it isn't in our nature. Even the best of us are falling with style.

Peter, not yet ready to give up on his let's-try-harder approach—and thus ignoring everything Jesus just said—wants to believe that he can contribute something to his salvation. He interrupts in verse 28, and essentially says, "Wait a minute, Jesus. We *did* that. We did exactly what you asked us to do. So why are you saying it's impossible? We've *done* it! We *have* left our homes, lands, families, and wealth. Haven't we earned eternal life?"

Let me summarize Jesus's response to Peter with an illustration: If I need to borrow ten dollars for lunch today and I promise to give you back twenty dollars tomorrow, would you be willing to loan me the ten dollars? Would someone "love" me enough to make that "sacrifice"? I'm sure your willingness to give me lunch money would have nothing to do with the ten dollars that your investment will return tomorrow.

That's the essence of Jesus's response to all Peter's "sacrifices" to live the Christian life. "Peter, what have you given up? You've gained houses and homes and land in this life, and in the life to come" (see Luke 18:29–30). There is nothing that we give up for Christ that isn't returned many times over.

Immediately after this story, Jesus speaks of his own death and resurrection. But why? Why would Jesus, after talking about salvation being impossible with man but possible with God, immediately talk about his death and resurrection? Because it is through the death and resurrection of Christ that God does what we cannot do. It's through Christ's death on the cross and resurrection that we, who are evil, are made good. It's by what Jesus has done for us, and not what we do for him, that puts us in a proper relationship with God, through Christ. The disciples, however, "understood none of these things. This saying was hidden from them, and they did not grasp what was said" (Luke 18:34).

The narrative becomes even more interesting because our next story is about a blind beggar. The blind man was sitting by the road when he heard a large crowd passing by and asked, "What's all the commotion about?" Someone answered, "Jesus of Nazareth is passing by" (Luke 18:37). He had heard about Jesus, and he knew that Jesus opened the eyes of the blind.

But it's not just the blind man who could not see. Jesus's own disciples were blind. Their blindness was spiritual, whereas the beggar's blindness was physical. The blind man began to shout, "Son of David, have mercy on me!" (Luke 18:39). The people around him told him to be quiet because they thought Jesus didn't want anything to do with him. But Jesus heard the blind man. Calling him forward, he opened his eyes.

To prove that only God makes us right with Him through Christ, we need to keep reading further. The next story, in Luke 19, is about Zacchaeus. Zacchaeus is a rich man. He's a *very* rich man. The principal difference between Zacchaeus and the rich man in chapter 18 is that the rich man is a very good man in his own right and in the eyes of those around him. Zacchaeus, because he is a tax collector, is a very bad man. If a rich good man cannot save himself, what are the chances of this rich, bad man being able to save himself?

But what happens to Zacchaeus? Jesus declares that he is a recipient of salvation. He has been made right with God by Jesus's declaration, "Today salvation has come to this house, since he also is a son of Abraham" (Luke 19:9). That's another way of saying that Zacchaeus has eternal life.

If I were the rich ruler, I would be angry at Jesus. I would say, "Wait a minute, Jesus, I object. Is the kingdom on sale today? Are you giving a 50 percent discount to this evil man? You asked me to give up everything to follow you, but you didn't ask Zacchaeus to give up *anything*. He just volunteered to give up half of all he owns and give back fourfold what he'd stolen (Luke 19:8), and you accepted that. How come you accepted only half from Zacchaeus, but from me you asked for everything?"

Jesus's concern was not the money, but the heart. What did Zacchaeus do to inherit eternal life? He welcomed Jesus joyfully (Luke 19:6). That's it.

Jesus's name in Hebrew means "salvation." Zacchaeus welcomed Jesus gladly. So when Jesus says, "salvation has come to this house," it is a play on words. Salvation has come to Zacchaeus's home because Jesus,

God's salvation, was gladly welcomed. Salvation has literally come, in the flesh, into Zacchaeus's home.

For further proof, let's look at the episode that takes place just *before* Jesus's encounter with the rich young ruler. In Luke 18:15, little children are being brought to Jesus and he's blessing them. The blind man couldn't get to Jesus because he was blind. Zacchaeus couldn't see Jesus because of his height, and he believed that because of his sin Jesus would have nothing to do with him. Likewise, the children have no chance of getting to Jesus unless someone brings them. Jesus says to his disciples, "Let the children come to me, and do not hinder them, for to such belongs the kingdom of God. Truly, I say to you, whoever does not receive the kingdom of God like a child shall not enter it" (Luke 18:16–17).

The children had a problem getting to Jesus; the blind man had a problem getting to Jesus; and Zacchaeus had a problem getting to Jesus. But who had *no* problem getting to Jesus? The rich man. The children, considered unimportant, were probably chased away so that Jesus could have this interview with this very important and wealthy man.

The children couldn't get to Jesus, the blind man couldn't get to Jesus, and Zacchaeus couldn't get to Jesus—but Jesus could get to them! As Jesus himself promised, "the Son of Man came to seek and to save the lost" (Luke 19:10).

The good news of the gospel is that you cannot get to Jesus, but he can get to you. He can hear you over the noise, he can see you through the crowd, and he saves his people.

What do we know about Zacchaeus, other than that he was a tax collector? He was little—just like children were little. Jesus just told us, "Whoever does not receive the kingdom of God like a child shall not enter it" (Luke 18:17). Not only was Zacchaeus childlike in his stature, he was also childlike in his behavior. What was Zacchaeus doing when Jesus found him? He had climbed a tree. When was the last time you climbed a tree? When you were a child. Zacchaeus did a very childlike thing: he climbed a tree just to see Jesus.

We may not have realized it, but Jesus has already introduced us to both the rich man and Zacchaeus—in Luke 18, in the parable of the Pharisee and the tax collector. Instead of creating a parable about two hypothetical people, Jesus very well could have actually *seen* these two men praying in the temple. He may have been there when they were praying—and later on answered each of their prayers. What did the rich ruler ask for? Nothing. He needed nothing, not a thing. He informed God of what a good job he was doing. "Look at me fly!"

What did the tax gatherer ask for? He prayed, "'God, be merciful to me, a sinner!'" (Luke 18:13). What did the blind man ask for? Mercy. He understood that he was crashing to the ground.

Are you beginning to see why it's grace from beginning to end? Our wooden wings and wooden tail are of no value. We are crashing to the ground because flying—even flying with style—is completely contrary to our nature. What we need is for God to give us mercy and grace so that Christ might do *through* us those things that are not *in* us.

Perhaps you're thinking, "I can never be a Christian. I've got too many bad habits that disqualify me." That's not true—unless you have the one bad habit of not asking Christ for mercy and for grace, unless you refuse to welcome Jesus gladly. It is Jesus that saves us. Jesus changes us. It's not us. Jesus is the answer to our prayers.

Perhaps you've been a Christian for a long time and still struggle. You believe that you can never change. Have you traded in Christ for a set of wooden wings and tail? Don't you know that what was begun by grace must be completed with grace? In Paul's words to the churches in Galatia, "I am astonished that you are so quickly deserting him who called you in the grace of Christ and are turning to a different gospel" (Galatians 1:6). There is another way to fly.

For my fortieth birthday, my wife and children decided they would give me a special gift. They had to tell me about the gift a couple of weeks before my birthday so we could prepare for it. My girls all gathered around me and said, "For your birthday, we want to take you parasailing!"

I responded, "Isn't that where you jump off a cliff with a parachute?"

And they said, "Yeah, Daddy, that'll be great!"

I said, trying to mask my fear, "I'm a simple man. Just a small party at home, with some friends and family, a cake, some candles—that's really all I need." What I meant was, *My only true desire is to make sure I celebrate my forty-first birthday.*

I was scared to death. I was even more frightened when I found out that my wife had taken out a life insurance policy! But I thought of a way out. The Bible says that the prayers of a righteous man avail much. Elijah prayed and it did not rain, and he prayed and it did rain (see James 5:17). I knew that if it rained we would have to cancel the plunge to my death. So I prayed it would rain.

The morning of my birthday was clear and dry with a crispness in the air. It was a beautiful day in southern France—perfect weather for crashing to the ground. *So much for the prayers of a righteous man,* I thought. We loaded up the car and began driving toward the mountains where I would do this thing. The entire time I was hoping that the car would break down or a tire would go flat—anything to get out of this predicament.

As we reached the top of the mountain and went through a tunnel, I looked up, and up again. There were cliffs! I knew that had to be where we were headed. There was no way I could do this.

I found the building where I was to sign up. I thought I had one last opportunity to get out of this. I told my family to stay in the car. This way I could go cancel my trip and tell them there was a problem and that I wouldn't be able to parasail today.

But as I entered the building, there was a young girl in front of me, about twelve or thirteen years of age. She was all excited, saying, "Where do I sign up? This is going to be fun!" The gentleman behind the table asked me my name, and as soon as I gave it to him he said, "Yes, you're all paid up. We just need you to sign this release and get in the van because we're ready to go." I figured I couldn't show how frightened I was in front of the French—after all, I *am* an American. So I said, "Can you explain to me what I am to do?"

"Just follow us to the van and we will explain everything on the trip up the mountain." I kissed my wife and three daughters goodbye— maybe it would be the last time—and got into the van.

I sat right behind the driver, tapping him on the shoulder and interrupting his conversation with his colleague. I said, "Can you tell me what I need to do?" He responded, "I'll tell you when we get up to the top," and he went back to talking to his friend. It was obvious he didn't want to be disturbed.

We pulled up to the top of this mountain. There was a grassy plain and then it dropped off about sixty yards from where the van was parked. I said again to the driver, "What do you want me to do?"

He said, "I need to get everybody set up. Why don't you just stand over there and wait for me?" as he pointed toward the cliff.

"Over *there*?" I asked.

"Yes, over there."

"How *far* over there?"

"Over there by the edge, but not too close. Just stand over there."

"OK," I halfheartedly responded.

After getting everyone else ready, the gentleman came over and laid out our parachute on the ground. I once more asked him, "What am I to do?" He handed me a harness and told me to put it on. "What do you want me to do *now*?" I asked.

He explained, "I'm going to clip my harness onto your harness and then I want you to lean forward and step off the cliff."

"Shouldn't I be behind you?"

"No, because I'm hooked into you," he said. "You simply lean forward and step off the cliff."

I asked, "What about my hands? What should I do with them?"

"Hold onto these ropes."

"Great!" I exclaimed. "Finally, something I get to do! What do holding onto these ropes do?"

"They keep your hands out of my face."

We edged forward, until I could see over the cliff. Then he said to me impatiently, "Lean forward and step off the cliff."

"Shouldn't we count to three or something?"

"No, just lean forward and step off the cliff," he repeated.

Closing my eyes, we leaned forward, causing the parachute to rise and fill with air. I stepped out, and we were immediately lifted off the ground. I opened my eyes and realized I wasn't crashing to my death, but was being carried upward by the thermal winds. As we banked to the left, continuing to rise, I could hear the swooshing of the wind as we were swept along the cliffs. The cliffs that looked so ominous from below, now close up were beautiful. You could see how the wind and weather had worn the rocks into beautiful shapes. You could even see birds nesting in the crags.

We banked right out over the valley. Below us were vineyards, lavender, and sunflower fields. A stream with the sun reflecting off it ran down the middle of the valley. I was caught up in the beauty of what I saw around me. Before I knew it, my hands, which had been white-knuckled and clinging to the ropes, had dropped to my side.

We banked again and came along the cliffs, then again soared back over the valley. It seemed like we were up there forever, floating effortlessly, endlessly, and then slowly descending. We touched the ground, where my family cheered.

That's salvation, Christ's way.

So you have a choice: you can strap on those wooden wings and tail and attempt the impossible—or you can entrust yourself to Christ, who will be able to do through you what you cannot do yourself. If you want what I have just described to be true in your life, then just simply do what Jesus asks. Lean forward and step off—repent and believe. Cry out to Jesus, "Lord, have mercy on me!"

But the above story isn't just for those who don't know Christ. It's really a story for those of us who *have* been walking with Christ. Because what we tend to do once the Lord gets us off the ground is take out our wooden wings and tail and let Jesus know that we'll take it from here. We begin flailing away, believing we're at least helping him out. But all our efforts are not adding one bit to what Christ has done for us. If anything, we're robbing him of his glory because in our foolishness we believe that we're making a real difference.

We must realize it is all Jesus and nothing of us and give him all the praise and glory. The Christian life is lived—from beginning to end—by grace. If we are going to share this message with others, we must first know it for ourselves.

Discussion Questions

1. Why does the "I can do it" mentality kill our ability to witness to others?

2. What do the children, the blind man, and Zacchaeus all have in common in Luke 18?

3. How are you tempted to rob Christ of his glory by thinking "I can do it"?

3

Luke 7: Christ's Method,
Our Model

As followers of Christ, we want to be sure that the content of our message is consistent with Jesus's message—but content isn't enough! We also want to be sure that our method is consistent with the message. Just as we look to Christ and his teaching for the content of our message, we must also look to him for how to deliver the message. The Gospels do this very thing. They not only tell us what message we are called to share; they teach us how to share our faith. Therefore, we can read ourselves into the gospel story as part of the twelve—part of the inner circle of disciples who are also learners at the feet of our Lord.

After spending the night alone in prayer, Jesus returns to his disciples and designates twelve as apostles (Luke 6:12–16). The twelve are beginning a new phase of training. They have moved from learners (disciples) to teachers—those sent out (apostles). Before sending them out, however—and at the beginning of Luke's rendering of the Sermon of the Mount (Luke 6:17–49), before a multitude of people—Jesus delivers a commencement address directly to the Twelve (Luke 6:17–22). They may be poor, hungry, mournful, and persecuted—but because they are all these things for Jesus's sake, they are blessed, and their reward will be great in heaven. Armed with this knowledge, Jesus now takes them—and us—on our first training exercise.

As we walk along, we wonder if we really need to take the words of Jesus's sermon literally. Does he *really* want us to turn the other cheek and loan our money without expecting anything back? Certainly, much of what he just said must be hyperbole! At least we *hope* it is.

As we enter Capernaum (Luke 7:1), it looks as if the toughest part of our job is going to be crowd control. We push our way through the crowd when we notice some very important people, the synagogue officials, headed toward us. They want to speak to Jesus. We can overhear what they are saying. They are explaining that a Roman centurion has a servant who is sick, and he wants Jesus to heal him. The synagogue officials explain that this is a very good man. He is worthy of Jesus granting his request because, as they say, he loves the Jews and he even built their synagogue for them.

Jesus doesn't ask us apostles what he should do, but we all have opinions. If you're morally minded, you're probably thinking, "Jesus, we should help this man because he is such a good person. These are the kind of people we should be helping—good people who live good lives." If you're politically minded you're thinking, "Jesus, we must help this man because you never know when we'll need a friend in high places. There are problems between the Jews and the Romans. A centurion could be of use to us." And if you're financially oriented, you're thinking, "Jesus, don't let this opportunity get away. The centurion is very wealthy. If we heal his servant, he will owe us. Then we can ask him to build *us* a synagogue too. We can get out of this itinerant ministry. We need cash for the poor. You can't feed the multitudes on a few loaves and fishes."

Jesus readily agrees to go with these leaders to the home of the centurion, but not for any of the reasons just mentioned. It is because Jesus is showing his apostles how to apply the teachings he just shared in Luke 6. In particular he is demonstrating what it means to live out his command in Luke 6:27, "Love your enemies." While the centurion was a good and generous Roman, the Romans in general were still enemies of the Jews, and the centurion was not exempt from this kind of racial hatred (or, at the very least, racial prejudice).

Why is it necessary for us, if we are going to share the gospel with others, to love our enemies? Because the gospel's central message is about God loving his enemies—which once included us. Paul writes, "while we were enemies we were reconciled to God by the death of his Son" (Romans 5:10). How can we profess that we have been transformed by a God who loved us even when we were his enemies, if *we* don't love *our* enemies? The only way the world will believe in such a God is if they see those of us who call him Lord loving our enemies.

Loving our enemies also teaches us that the gospel is bigger and more important than any other issue. It trumps all divisions, prejudices, and hatred. The gospel is more important than any personal or political issues you may have with others.

It's nice to minister to the wealthy and well-connected, but in order that we don't get too comfortable with the rich and influential, Jesus quickly moves us along on our journey.

The next person we meet "soon afterward" (Luke 7:11) is a widow. The story of the centurion and the widow are thus connected temporally, but there is also an ironic thematic connection between these two stories. Much is made of the centurion's worthiness by the Jewish leaders. In Luke 7:6, the centurion declares that he is *not* worthy—which makes him all the more worthy because he is that rare person of wealth and power who is also humble.

In the Greek text of Luke 7 there are two different words used for "worthy." The word ἄξιός (*axios*) is used in Luke 7:4 by the Jewish leaders to describe the centurion, and ἱκανός (*hikanos*) is used by the centurion in Luke 7:6 to describe himself. The word ἱκανός is only used three times in Luke's Gospel. Two of those times are in chapter 7—once when the centurion describes himself as not being "worthy," and again in verse 12. The worthiness of the widow is the "considerable"—literally, "worthy" (ἱκανός)—crowd attending her son's funeral. Luke wants to make sure we see that these two stories are linked.

On a human scale, the centurion and the widow have nothing in common. In fact they are on the opposite ends of a spectrum of humanity. Everything that the centurion is, the widow is not. He is male; she is female. He is rich; she is poor. In the Bible, widows are invariably poor; Jesus tells us about the widow's two mites, while James commands us to visit widows and orphans in their distress (James 1:27). The centurion is a Gentile; the widow is a Jew. He is powerful and influential; the widow is weak and powerless. The widow in the parable of Luke 18 can't even get what's rightfully hers, begging the judge until he tires of her. Only then does she get justice. The centurion is asking Jesus's help for a slave he can live without. The woman just lost everything she had—her son. These two are opposites on almost every level, two extremes on a human scale.

These two stories represent the first dimension of those who Christ calls us to. We can think of this as the horizontal, human dimension that every person falls onto somewhere. The next two people we meet in Luke 7 fall on a vertical dimension—a spiritual plane.

Starting in Luke 7:18, we encounter a delegation sent by John the Baptist; John cannot come because he is in prison. Jesus says about John, "among those born of women none is greater than John" (Luke 7:28). On a spiritual scale, John the Baptist is at the top. He is the best that flesh and blood can produce. And yet, even John's eyes and those of his disciples need to be opened further.

> In that hour he healed many people of diseases and plagues and evil spirits, and on many who were blind he bestowed sight. And

he answered them, "Go and tell John what you have seen and heard: the blind receive their sight, the lame walk, lepers are cleansed, and the deaf hear, the dead are raised up, the poor have good news preached to them. And blessed is the one who is not offended by me." (Luke 7:21–23)

Again, John the Baptist represented the very top of humanity, spiritually speaking. Near the bottom was a woman—the last person Jesus introduces us to in Luke 7, "who was a sinner" (Luke 7:37) and generally assumed to be a prostitute. And yet, there is another person in this story who is even lower than this woman. He believes that he should be near the top of humanity, but according to Jesus he is at the bottom. For just below the sinful woman is a self-righteous man, Simon the Pharisee. It is interesting that we're given his name, but not hers. Why is Simon just below the prostitute? Because according to this account, "he who is forgiven little, loves little" (Luke 7:47).

In the encounter with the prostitute, Jesus demonstrates another example of what it means to live out his teachings in Luke 6. The way Jesus treats the sinful woman takes us back to Luke 6:37—"Judge not, and you will not be judged; condemn not, and you will not be condemned"—and shows us how to apply it.

Simon condemns the woman *and* Jesus. Yet Jesus shows her mercy. When Jesus commands us to "judge not," it doesn't mean we cannot sit on a jury and determine someone's guilt or innocence. It *does* mean that we do not determine in advance who is worthy or unworthy of God's grace.

But wait, isn't "worthy grace" an oxymoron? That's Jesus's point— it is only grace if you *aren't* worthy of it. If we're going to share a gospel of grace, then we cannot decide who is and who is not worthy of God's grace. God revealed himself to Moses as the God who "will be gracious to whom I will be gracious, and will show mercy on whom I will show mercy" (Exodus 33:19). This means that we never count *anyone* outside the reach of God's mercy and grace.

On our training exercise with Jesus, he introduces us to a centurion, a widow, a prophet, and a prostitute. I call these people the four compass points of humanity, because you cannot find four people who are more different from one another. After hearing about these four people—these four extremes of the human condition—your heart should begin to rejoice. If the grace of God can touch a Roman centurion, a Jewish widow, a prophet, and a prostitute, his grace can touch your life as well. The good news of the gospel is that no one is outside the reach of God's grace and mercy. You are not too rich or too poor, too good or too bad, too powerful or weak, or so spiritual or so sinful that the grace of God in Jesus Christ cannot touch your life.

There is also an important application for the church. By taking us to the extremes of humanity, Jesus is teaching us that we are to offer the gospel to everyone. Regardless of our differences as human beings, we all have the same need—which can only be answered by the gospel.

Christ's example in Luke 7 flies in the face of conventional wisdom on church planting. In the last half of the twentieth century we have been taught that if you want to plant a church you should get people together who are the same. That is, if you put together people from the same ethnic, economic, and educational background, you will plant fast-growing churches. If you can get people together who think, act, and look alike, that will draw other people who are just like them. This is known as the homogeneous unit principle, and it really works. But demographics, not the power of the gospel, is its true driving force. You can start churches this way—or clubs, civic organizations, or any given social group.

However, there's something contradictory about the homogeneous unit principle and what Jesus is teaching us in Luke 7. Not only are we to preach the gospel to all kinds of people, we are to expect that some of these very different people will believe the gospel and become part of a local fellowship of believers. The church of Jesus Christ is unique because of its diversity. Too many churches are built on sociological principles, rather than the gospel. The only explanation for Christ's church is that all these diverse people are held together by their common allegiance to our Lord. Even former enemies are now brothers and sisters in Christ because of his gospel.

It is because of the church's diversity that the followers of Christ were first called Christians in Antioch. You could not call them Jews or Gentiles, for both were in the church. You could not label them wealthy or poor, intellectuals or idiots, because the church was made up from all categories of humanity. The only thing that all these diverse people had in common was Christ, and therefore that was the only title you could give them: Christians.

Jesus not only shows us to whom we are to minister in Luke 7 but *how* we are to minister. Have you ever noticed that Jesus just loved to irritate the "heaven" out of the Pharisees? He just seemed to intentionally do things that would get under their skin. We see Jesus doing this throughout Luke 7 because he wants his disciples—you and me—to be different from the Pharisees. He must stress this over and over again because being a Pharisee comes all too naturally to us. Christ, in Luke 7, is showing his disciples that the way they are to serve God is completely different from the way the Pharisees "serve God." What *is* that difference?

The Pharisees believed that to serve God, they must keep themselves pure and clean from the dirty things in this world—especially "dirty people." In the parable of the Good Samaritan, the priest and the Levite would not help the man left for dead because if he were dead and they touched him they would immediately become unclean. Forget the fact that they were going down from Jerusalem—which meant that their service at the temple was done. At best, the Pharisees believed that they were serving God by keeping themselves spiritually clean. At worst, they placed a wedge between the first table of the Law (loving God) and the second table of the Law (loving man)—to play one off the other, and thereby keeping neither.

We all do this. We say we are serving God, but do it in such a way that it keeps us from serving our fellow man. In Luke 7, Jesus shows us that this is not the way we are to be his apostles. He teaches us that to preach the gospel we must do the exact opposite of what the Pharisees did. We must be willing to become dirty for the sake of the gospel. This is how he calls us to serve him. Let's revisit what he teaches us in Luke 7.

In the first story, Jesus is asked to go to the home of a Gentile, the Roman centurion, and heal his servant. Jesus agrees to the request and follows the centurion's envoys. The question everybody is asking is not whether Jesus can heal the sick servant; that's not what a Jew would be concerned about. The real concern is whether Jesus will go into this Gentile's home. Jews did not go into the home of Gentiles because if they did they became unclean. You see this in the passion narratives when Jesus is taken to Pilate's home. The chief priest and his delegation will not enter his dwelling because they don't want to become defiled and unable to eat the Passover meal (John 18:28).

Sometime later, when Peter was sent to the first Gentile in the book of Acts, who was also a Roman centurion, the only thing the people back in Jerusalem confronted Peter with was, "You went to uncircumcised men and ate with them" (Acts 11:3).

Jesus was on the way to the home of a Gentile—big problem. He didn't go in, but he was willing to go. The centurion knew what he was asking of Christ. This is why he stopped Jesus, saying, "I am not worthy to have you come under my roof" (Luke 7:6). Nonetheless, Jesus was willing to become unclean by going into the home of a Gentile.

In the second story, the son of the widow is being carried out for burial. I believe that when Jesus saw this widow he thought about his own mother and burial. Jesus goes over and touches the coffin (Luke 7:14). Did Jesus need to touch the coffin to raise the man? No;

when he raised Lazarus, he just shouted from a distance. He didn't have to touch the coffin, but he did. At that point Jesus became ceremonially unclean according to the Mosaic Law (Numbers 19:11).

Jesus takes another step down into the sinfulness and sickness of man in the next story. The disciples of John the Baptist come and ask, "Are you the one who is to come, or shall we look for another?" (Luke 7:19). Jesus answers the question by telling them to watch. And in that very hour he heals the sick, the blind, the lame, and even lepers. Earlier in Luke, it says that Jesus actually touched sick people when he healed them (Luke 5:13). It doesn't say that he touched sick people in this passage, but touching those he healed was a regular part of Jesus's ministry. We can conclude that Jesus touched some of the sick people mentioned in Luke 7.

Jesus was willing to go to the home of a Gentile, to touch the coffin of a dead man, and now he is actually touching live sick people. But it doesn't stop there. Jesus takes another step down. When Jesus is eating dinner at Simon's home, a prostitute enters and begins touching Jesus. Simon asks the right question, doesn't he? "If this man were a prophet, he would have known who and what sort of woman this is who is touching him, for she is a sinner" (Luke 7:39).

We all would like to know why Jesus is allowing himself to be touched by a prostitute. You don't have to be a prophet to recognize a prostitute; anybody can. But Simon was right in asking why a holy man was allowing himself to be touched by this dirty woman. And what is she touching our Savior with? She is using the tools of her trade—her hands and her lips. Where had those hands and lips been? Why should anyone like her be allowed near the Lord? But before we condemn her, we must realize that our hands and mouth are no cleaner than hers.

I am sorry to be so graphic, but we sanitize the Bible and don't see the ugliness of real life. The Bible is R-rated, but we want to read it as if it were family-friendly! If we sanitize the Scripture so Jesus only forgives good people with not-so-bad sins, then we do ourselves a disservice. We need to know our Lord forgives really ugly and dirty sin—so that we know we are truly forgiven of all the terrible and ugly things we have done.

The sinful woman then takes out a vial of alabaster perfume. I call this the "vile vial" because it represents this woman's life of prostitution and all she has gained from it. Even though it smells beautiful and is very expensive—it represents approximately a year's salary to a common laborer—in reality it stinks like hell.

What happens next is one of the clearest examples of repentance, faith, and justification. The sinful woman empties the vial onto the feet of Jesus. She pours out her life of prostitution—literally, "the wages of sin"—on Jesus. She is repenting of all of it. By emptying the vial, she is placing all her sin on Jesus. Then Jesus declares her forgiven (Luke 7:48).

Paul says it this way in 2 Corinthians 5:21, "For our sake he made him to be sin who knew no sin, so that in him we might become the righteousness of God." Jesus stepped down into the sinfulness of this world, bearing our infirmities, sickness, and sin. He took them on himself for our healing. Jesus stepped down even further when he went to the cross and bore the sin of the world. So disturbing was this to the cosmos that the sky became dark and the earth shook.

I love Psalm 40 where David writes: "He drew me up from the pit of destruction, out of the miry bog, and set my feet upon a rock, making my steps secure. He put a new song in my mouth" (Psalm 40:2–3). I like how the NIV translates it: "He lifted me out of the slimy pit."

If you had to get someone out of a slimy pit, how would you do it? I'd probably begin by shouting at him, "Hey you, don't you know you're in a slimy pit? *Get out of there!*" That is what so much of evangelism is—telling people what they already know. They will never admit it to us, though—particularly when we're shouting at them.

If that didn't work I would throw him a rope. "Grab hold and I'll pull you out," I would offer. But the Bible says that we're dead in our trespasses and sins, and dead people don't grab hold of ropes too well. If I had to get him out, I would look for the cleanest part and grab hold of it with one hand, while keeping the rest of his dirty stinking body as far away from me as possible. I would shake him off with one hand and tell him to sing. That is how *I* would get someone out of a slimy pit.

But do you know how Jesus saves sinners? The Bible says that "though he was in the form of God, [he] did not count equality with God a thing to be grasped, but emptied himself, by taking the form of a servant, being born in the likeness of men" (Philippians 2:6–7). You see, Jesus climbed down into that vile pit. He knelt down beside me, wrapping his arms around my lifeless body; he took my dirty head into his pure hands, and he placed his pure lips over my filthy mouth and breathed into me the Holy Spirit. That's how God saves sinners.

Do you know why the world has stopped listening to the gospel? Because we want to share it in the least inconvenient, least costly way. We want to save dirty people at a distance.

The church has missed wonderful opportunities to show the radical love of Christ for sinners in my lifetime. The first was the AIDS epidemic. I remember being in churches that discussed, "Well, what if a child with AIDS came to our nursery? What would we do? We can't allow that." And I say if there's no place for AIDS victims in the church, then there's no place for the church in this world. Because if they can't find hope there, where will they find it? Another place where the church is missing a wonderful opportunity is in the abortion debates. When a young girl leaves part of herself in an abortion clinic, what does she need most? She needs to be loved and forgiven. Now where's the only place she's going to find that? It should be in the church. But where's the last place she'll go for help? The church. Christ is calling us not just to talk about God's love for sinners, but to actually step down into the world and show it.

But that's our problem, isn't it? We have been all cleaned up. We stand, looking down into that dirty pit. Christ asks us to step down into it with him, but we don't want to. There is nothing in us that desires to go back down there. But who needs Jesus Christ the most *now*—the people in the pit or those of us who are standing paralyzed, unable to step down again into it?

What we need is the same thing the people in the pit need—grace, repentance, and faith. We *all* need the gospel, *always*.

During the years we worked in France we met all kinds of Muslims. Most of them are very friendly, kind, and loving people, but occasionally we would meet some angry Muslims. One morning on a university campus, while a small group of people were gathered around listening to my colleague answer questions about Christianity, a young man pushed his way into the group and immediately began verbally attacking my coworker. He kept saying how Christians were his enemies, and that he would fight and kill them.

Everyone was frightened by this man's demeanor. Some people walked away, while others came running over to see what all the commotion was about. For some reason, however, I decided to go stand right beside him. I took his arm in mine—the gesture of close friendship. He pulled it away and kept shouting. I took his arm again. He didn't pull it away this time but continued shouting. "We are going to fight you Christians wherever we find you."

In a raised voice I replied, "But we are going to love you! We are not going to take anyone's life, but lay down our lives for the good of others. We are going to forgive those who persecute us and turn the other cheek." This went on for a few minutes until I think he realized how he was embarrassing both Islam and himself. When he quieted down, I asked his name and whether he would like to have a drink with me. Amar and I never agreed, but we did have a much more civil discussion over coffee. And in that conversation, Amar heard about—and hopefully saw—the love of Jesus.

It's remarkable that each time Jesus steps down and identifies with sinners and their suffering there is a corresponding elevation and revelation of who Jesus Christ is. If I were God and wanted to prove it to the world, I might do it by some big flashy event—maybe write my name in the sky. But God chooses to do it by identifying with the suffering and the sinful—identifying with *us*.

It's ironic that the very thing that is most often used to prove there is no all-powerful and good God—suffering—is the very way that God chooses to reveal himself to us.

In the story of the centurion, Jesus is willing to go to his house but doesn't have to. What do we learn about Jesus? That he is better than the local healer because he can heal at a distance.

In the next story, when Jesus steps down by touching the coffin of the widow's son and raises him, people say about him, "A great prophet has arisen among us!" (Luke 7:16). The great prophet who came to the people's minds was Elijah. He too raised a widow's son. Jesus is now not only a healer; he's also a prophet like Elijah, the forerunner of the Messiah.

When John the Baptist sends his men to ask, "Are you the one who is to come" (Luke 7:20)—meaning, are you the Messiah?—Jesus reveals himself to John's men by touching and healing sick people. Then he tells John's disciples, "Go and tell John what you have seen and heard: the blind receive their sight, the lame walk, lepers are cleansed, and the deaf hear, the dead are raised up, the poor have good news preached to them" (Luke 7:22). Thus, Jesus's status is raised again: from healer, to great prophet, to Messiah.

In the last story, when Jesus is being touched by the prostitute and says to her, "Your sins are forgiven," the people around the tables whisper what no one would dare say out loud: "Who is this, who even forgives sins?" (Luke 7:49). The unspoken answer is that Jesus is God.

Then on the cross, when our Lord was dying, another Roman centurion who must have seen many Jews crucified saw something different in the death of this Jew. As he witnessed the suffering and dying of Christ, what did he say? "Truly this was the Son of God!" (Matthew 27:54).

Do you want the world to take notice of the gospel? Then do what Christ did—identify with the sick, suffering, and dying. People can build big churches, but does that point people to God? I've visited Notre Dame Cathedral in Paris, and when I go there I don't think, *God is great!* I think, *What a building!* It's a monument to the people who built it. A monument that brings glory to God is one where we give our lives daily in service to others.

There was a missionary named Joseph Damian who served in Hawaii. Tough spot—Hawaii. But he served on the island of Molokai, at the leper colony.

When leprosy arrived in the Hawaiian Islands, those who contracted it were treated cruelly. They were rounded up and dumped on the island of Molokai, on a sandbar that formed a natural prison with the ocean on one side and the mountains on the other. The crews on the ships that carried the lepers would make them jump into the ocean and swim ashore, throwing their belongings overboard as well. The doctors visiting the lepers would examine them from across the room and leave the medicine on the table, making them wait till after they left to retrieve it.

When Joseph Damian arrived he found people simply waiting to die, living like animals with no hope. Instead, he washed and bandaged their wounds, built a church, started a choir, and helped people plant gardens. He served them faithfully for years.

One morning, when he was preparing his morning cup of tea, he spilled some hot water on his toes, but he felt nothing. He then took the teapot and poured hot water over his feet, but still there was no sensation. He had worked with lepers long enough to know the diagnosis.

That morning he addressed his people with these words: "We lepers." At that moment, his congregation understood the work of Christ in a brand new way. They could understand how God loved them so much that he sent his Son to bear their infirmities and to take on their sickness so that they might be made well.

In Statuary Hall in the House of Representatives, each state has the right to choose two statues that represent the best ideals of their state. Hawaii sent their two statues. The first statue is of the Hawaiian king Kamehameha I, who is believed to be divine because he descended from the gods and heaven. The second statue is of the missionary Joseph Damian, in whom they saw the Divine at work by stepping down into the sin, sickness, and suffering of mankind.

Discussion Questions

1. Why is loving your enemy critical to the gospel message? Why is not judging others critical to the gospel message?

2. Did you find the observation that the prostitute was touching our Lord with the tools of her trade offensive? Why do we tend to downplay the sinfulness of this woman? How can we step down with Jesus into the sin, sickness, and suffering of this world?

3. Is it important that the church be as diverse as the community in which it is found? How can you work toward your church being as diverse as the community in which it is found?

A Real Approach
to Sharing the Gospel

4

For Christ's Sake, Be Normal

"I have a problem," began the young lady as she took a seat in my office. "My sister is coming to live with me and her life is always just one step away from tragedy. If anyone needs Christ, my sister does."

She continued, "We used to be close when we were younger, but then we went our separate ways. I became a believer and she became a skeptic; she completely rejected the faith we both grew up in. We haven't had a lot of contact the last few years, but now she is coming to live with me! I'm worried; I'm worried because I want to share my hope with her, but how can I when I struggle so much and am filled with doubts and questions myself? How can I speak boldly about my faith?"

"Why don't you begin," I responded, "by telling her about your doubts? Tell her about the struggles you have."

"I can't do that!" she gasped. "I want her to believe. I want her to know the truth of the gospel."

"So you want your skeptical sister to believe in a way that you yourself do *not* believe?" I asked. "Have you ever considered that the way you present yourself as a Christian might be *part* of the reason your sister doesn't believe? Non-Christians are often more honest than we are. Perhaps she sees in you someone who never questions, doubts, or struggles. What she may be rejecting is something she believes is unobtainable for her—a faith that is either blind or naïve. Instead of being a help to your sister, you may be her biggest obstacle to belief because she can never imagine herself believing like the person you want *her* to believe *you* are.

"Why don't you try being normal, for Christ's sake? Share your doubt and struggles with her. Let her know that you're a bit of a skeptic yourself. But also share how good the Lord is to you in the midst of those difficulties and how he is your strength, even in your doubting."

We all have family members, friends, and neighbors we want to share the gospel with. Perhaps you had someone in particular in mind when you picked up this book. And yet you feel that you can't be honest with them about your own struggles and doubts because that would somehow weaken the gospel.

However, the opposite is true. When we're not honest about our struggles and our faith, we distort the gospel, and in fact may be putting false barriers in the way of those we are so anxious to bring to Christ. We want people to see Jesus in us when it would be so much better if they instead saw someone *in need of* Jesus.

Therefore, for Christ's sake, be *normal!*

Christians, too often, live under the guilt of not being "Christian enough." We all believe that if we were better, people would see the Lord in us, and they would give their lives to Christ. The truth is that our example to those who know us best is not what we would like it to be. Therefore we overcompensate in two ways: either we try harder to be Christian, or we witness more to those we love. Thank God our nonbelieving family and friends really do love us because they keep putting up with us.

In our desire to show others how different we are because of Christ, we're not making ourselves any more appealing to the nonbelievers around us. In fact, we are presenting ourselves as weird, strange, and bizarre.

So stop it! For Christ's sake, be normal. When we're normal and open about our difficulties and struggles, Christ in all his power and glory will come pouring out of the cracks in our lives. With non-Christians, we must go so far out of our way to be normal that *we* are the uncomfortable ones. We must work at being normal so that others can imagine themselves being able—and by God's grace, deeply desire—to be followers of Jesus.

When we were missionaries, we had prayer cards. There are three frightening things about a prayer card: 1) If people knew what we have to go through to get one good picture of our family with everyone smiling, their eyes open and looking at the camera, they'd be horrified. 2) The picture itself. I think you can find them all on awkwardfamilyphotos.com. 3) The Bible verse that is prominently displayed on the front of the card.

Just under our family's smiling faces was our verse. Most people choose a verse everyone knows, but we chose a verse that no one knows and most people can't even remember reading. Our verse was 2 Corinthians 5:13: "If we are out of our mind, it is for the sake of God; if we are in our right mind, it is for you" (NIV 1984). We chose this verse because it describes exactly what I mean when I say, "For Christ's sake, be normal."

Paul describes loving God as being "out of our minds" for him, or "crazy!" When I was dating my wife I remember telling her, "I'm crazy about you." Love does make you do some very crazy things. How do we show our love for our Savior? Jesus says, "If you love me, you will keep my commandments" (John 14:15). We show our love for God by doing what he asks and desires of us. That is all we have to do for the people around us to think we're crazy, absolutely out of our minds.

When we prepared to work with Muslims in 1988, everyone who heard about us leaving the U.S. said, "Are you crazy?" Now it doesn't have to be anything as big as that; it can be small acts of devotion for our Lord that make those around us look at us as if we're crazy. If a friend asks you to do something on a Sunday and you decline by saying, "I have church," she immediately asks, "Are you crazy?" If you decline to engage in certain types of behavior and your friends press you for the reason, and you admit, "I won't because I'm a Christian," their response is, "Are you crazy?"

Don't feel badly if people call you crazy—this just proves that you're in good company! They said it about Jesus when they listened to his teaching: "He has a demon, and is insane" (John 10:20). Festus said to Paul after hearing his defense of the gospel, "Paul, you are out of your mind; your great learning is driving you out of your mind" (Acts 26:24). All it takes for the world to believe that we're crazy is for us to follow the teachings of our Lord.

In 2 Corinthians 5:13, Paul explains that if we are going to be representatives of the gospel, we must keep two dimensions of our life in balance—our relationship with God and our relationship with others. It is Paul's way of summarizing the two great commandments: love God with all our hearts, and love our neighbors as ourselves.

The first relationship we must keep in balance is our relationship with God—that is, being out of our minds or crazy for him. We should think of this relationship as a vertical scale that can be divided into two parts. Either we are crazy for God, or we are not crazy. If being crazy for God is living a life of faith, being "not crazy" is where your faith makes no difference in your daily life.

The second relationship that Paul addresses is our relationship to others—a horizontal scale. Again, he describes the proper balance with others as being "in our right mind . . . for you." The single word that best describes what Paul means is "normal." Just as the vertical scale can be divided into two sections, the horizontal scale can also be divided into two sections. We can either be "normal" or "not normal." We can diagram what Paul is trying to teach us in the following way:

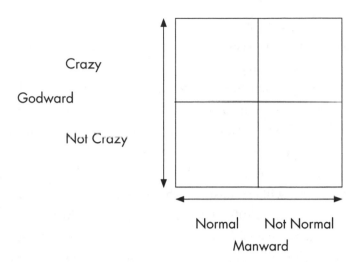

The result is that we can express our Christian faith in four differ-ent ways, three of which can negatively affect our witness before those around us. Let's look at the different ways we can live out our faith in these two relationships.

The first way (bottom left) is to be "not crazy" in our relation-ship with God, but to be completely "normal" with those around us. In other words, there is no difference in the way we live our lives from the non-Christians around us. We are so normal that our non-Christian friends have no idea that we are Christians—because there is no evidence of a living faith. Those of us who fit into this category are often referred to as nominal Christians. If your life falls into this category, you are having no impact on others because there is no evi-dence of what God can do in your life.

The second group (bottom right) is made up of those who are "not crazy" and "not normal." There is no evidence of faith in their spiritual lives, but at the same time these people are just weird. When my daughters were in high school they called people who fit this group "geeks" or "nerds." They are the kind of people who make you uncomfortable just being around them. They lack any social graces, don't know how to dress, and don't know how to act around others.

They believe people are avoiding them because they're Christian, but people don't even necessarily know they're Christian. People avoid them because they are *weird*.

The third group (top right)—"crazy" but "not normal"—is the choice that most of us believe is the proper way to live the Christian life. We have a relationship with God that is evident; we have a faith that impacts our daily lives; and we are different from the world around us. But this is not the balance that Paul is setting before us. Two examples will demonstrate what I mean.

On October 2, 2006, Charles Roberts killed five Amish girls in their one-room school house in Pennsylvania. The killings shocked the nation. But what captivated all of us was the way the Amish community responded, as they spoke of forgiveness and reconciliation. The Amish even set up a charitable fund for the shooter's family. There were articles written about how exemplary the Amish people were. They were held up as the standard of what all of us should strive to be. But did anyone become Amish because of their exemplary lives? Nonetheless, they are admired because of their commitment to follow Christ's teachings; they are "crazy" because their faith is evident in their daily lives.

The problem is that they are not normal. People didn't consider becoming Christians because of all the "not normal" or "weird" ways the Amish live. Who wants to wear black and those funny hats all the time, drive a horse-drawn buggy, and not have electricity, computers, or phones in their homes? No one! What the Amish have done is made a lot of nonessential things essential to the Christian faith by freezing in time a way of living that they believe best expresses what it means to be Christian.

But the Amish are not alone. Christians of all kinds have made nonessential things essential to the gospel in order to differentiate themselves from the world. But this does not help challenge those around us to give their lives to Christ. It only makes us and Christianity strange to non-Christians.

Paul speaks against this issue in Colossians when he says, "These [rules we have added to the gospel] have indeed an appearance of wisdom in promoting self-made religion and asceticism and severity to the body, but they are of no value in stopping the indulgence of the flesh" (Colossians 2:23). When we make a pronouncement to the world around us that we are different because of the nonessential things that we have added to the gospel, the world rolls its eyes because they can see that these things don't really matter, and in the things that do matter most of the time, we are no different than they are. Christ calls us to take up our cross by doing the uncomfortable thing of being normal—that is, not weird.

A second example of those who are "crazy" and "not normal" are those who try to be super-spiritual. For example, I don't know anyone who doesn't admire and revere Mother Teresa for her selfless serving of the poor, sick, and dying in Kolkata. Most of us can never be this super-spiritual, because everyday life gets in the way. Our time must be taken up in the mundane duties of providing for our families and church. And yet, there are those who feel they have to make themselves do something as extreme as travel to the other end of the world, or egregiously "manifest" some "spiritual gift" until they're sure the rest of us know they have it.

However, it is not these super-spiritual examples who generally have the greatest impact on non-Christians. It is those of us who have to live what are considered ordinary lives, but who live them for Christ.

It is the fourth category (top left) that most impacts the world. These people have a relationship with Christ that makes them different—"crazy" to the people around them— but who, at the same time, go out of their way to *not* be weird. They work hard at being like their neighbors in the nonessentials, so that people can imagine that they too can be followers of Christ in the essentials.

This is what our Lord did. He became like us so that we could become like him. He did the hard work, the uncomfortable work, and gave us an example to follow. We should do the hard work, keeping the balance of being crazy for God, but completely normal around others.

To be normal and not weird we must go out of our way to be interested in the things that most interest others. Why? Because it shows that we are deeply interested in them. Like our Lord, we do not use being normal around others as an excuse to sin, but as a way of giving others the opportunity to see what being a Christian is really like. This is the freedom that the gospel gives us. At the same time, we take Paul's warning to heart not to use this freedom as an opportunity for the flesh, but as an act of devotion to Christ and service to others (Galatians 5:13).

One way to apply this principle is when celebrating holidays. In my opinion, if you're interested in reaching your neighbors, one of the most important holidays to participate in, for Christ's sake, is Halloween. One reason is that it's the one night of the year that you can go and knock on all your neighbors' doors, and they will be happy to see you!

We moved into our home in early October 2000, and at the end of that month I went out with our girls trick-or-treating. My wife stayed at home, passing out candy. At the end of the evening we had met most everyone in our neighborhood.

We did not go to any of the extremes you see today. When our girls were little, we encouraged them to be princesses and butterflies, and once one wanted to be a turtle. But we have also had a zombie or two during the teenage years. We had a couple of carved pumpkins on the porch. Another idea to get people together around Halloween is to have a neighborhood pumpkin-carving for the children and follow it up with a pumpkin-pie party the next night. This kind of thing changes living on a street to living in a neighborhood.

We are always generous with the candy too, because I remember as a child that neighbors had reputations of being cheap or unfriendly by how much and what kind of candy they gave us. The worst were people we knew were at home, but who turned out all the lights so no one would bother them. Then there were those homes we looked forward to because they didn't just hand out the candy from behind a half-closed door, but they either invited us in or came out on the porch and engaged us in conversation. They gave us great candy, and lots of it.

I am not against passing out Bibles and tracts—just don't do it on Halloween, especially instead of giving out candy. It isn't what people are expecting, and you cheapen the faith by doing so.

There are real Satan worshipers who consider Halloween a "low unholy day," but what you will learn as you meet your neighbors is more frightening—they don't even believe there *is* a devil. So why make Halloween about him? Make All Hallow's Eve an opportunity to show the neighborhood that the new family on the block is just normal folk and a great addition to the neighborhood.

This could lead to neighborhood Super Bowl parties, annual block parties, and dinners with the neighbors. Each of these can become an opportunity to allow our Christian faith to leak out so that our neighbors can see we are crazy but normal, thus giving us opportunities to speak into their lives.

Discussion Questions

1. As Christians, what are some ways we present ourselves that make it difficult for others to become followers of Christ?

2. Can we be normal toward our fellow man without compromising the gospel? Why do we have difficulty finding proper balance?

3. Are evangelicals starting to look like the Amish to our culture? How? And what should we do about it?

5

Party Evangelism

When I ask North Americans what means the most to them about their relationship with Christ, the most common responses are forgiveness, joy, peace, eternal life, and that heaven is a free gift. If you were to categorize each of these answers under the headings of personal or communal, you would see that almost everyone is thinking individually. *I* am thankful that my sins are forgiven. *I* am grateful for the joy and peace that is in me. *I* cherish the eternal life that *I* have.

Not only do we think almost exclusively of our salvation as an individual benefit, we think of it as internal and spiritual. That is, our faith is lived out in us, in our private internal world. All of these responses need no tangible manifestation in the physical world. We can diagram these responses in the following way:

	Individual	Communal
Internal/Spiritual	Forgiveness Joy Peace Eternal Life	
External/Physical		

Western Christians live out their faith primarily in an individual and internal fashion. However, when I study the Scriptures, they seem to place the weight of the expression of the Christian faith on the communal and physical. This doesn't mean the Bible isn't calling us as individuals to repent and believe, or that our faith doesn't touch all these areas of our life, but the gospel impacts and changes more than my individual life. It builds a community, a people, and a society. Our Lord himself said, "I will build my church." That means our faith must produce communal and external fruit in the real world. We can diagram the difference in the following way:

	Individual	Communal
Internal/Spiritual	Western Christianity	
External/Physical		Scripture's emphasis

When culture is confused with what the Bible teaches, we call this confusion *syncretism*. It is easy to recognize syncretism in other cultures, particularly when Christianity and animistic religion are seamlessly woven together. I grew up in Miami, surrounded by a Hispanic Catholic community, some of whom were also involved in Santeria. Religious stores along Calle Ocho sold both Catholic saints and Santeria saints. They would pray in the church and sacrifice chickens on a street corner in Santeria rituals. This kind of syncretism is easy to identify. It is harder, though, to recognize it in our own culture and in our own lives. The syncretism that confuses the gospel with American culture and secular values is much harder for us to see because we're the ones doing it. It's the "not seeing the log in your own eye" syndrome.

The syncretism of our faith to our cultural values is both positive and negative. It is positive because Christianity can be lived out in unique ways in every culture. Our faith is not relative to culture, but our culture does impact the way we apply our faith. For example, it is just as Christian to sit quietly in a cathedral and follow a liturgy that never changes as it is to meet outdoors where people sing and dance and don't know what might come next. Shaping our faith by the culture so that it doesn't seem foreign or strange, but at home, is called contextualization.

The syncretism of our faith to our cultural values is negative when our cultural values distort or negate biblical values. Western Christianity distorts the gospel because the influence of individualism blinds us to Scripture's continual emphasis on the community.

We even read our cultural value of individualism into the text of the Bible, and the English language doesn't help us. In English the second person pronoun (you) is the same in the singular and the plural. The result is that many people read the "yous" in Scripture as though they apply to them individually.

For example, in 1 Corinthians 3:16 Paul writes, "Do you not know that you are God's temple and that God's Spirit dwells in you?" As Western Christians, we interpret this verse to mean that we should take care of our individual bodies by eating right, not smoking or doing drugs, and exercising. But Paul is not asking us to exercise. He is concerned about the health of the entire church and the fact that it has been compromised by divisions.

Western individualism has also distorted the gospel. Every gospel presentation that I know of emphasizes one's personal relationship with Christ, while at the same time saying nothing about the importance of the church. Some presentations will list for believers those things they should do to grow as a Christian. This is the first and only place most gospel presentations mention the church. The church, in these presentations, is not an essential and is at best optional. Therefore, we have many people in the West who think of themselves as Christians because they believe they have a personal relationship with Christ, and yet see no need at all to be part of a local church. The impact of our individual and internal gospel is seen in the devaluation of the church because we don't need anyone else, and certainly not the church, if the gospel is only about getting into heaven.

This message comes across loud and clear in the titles of two of my favorite country-western songs: "Me and Jesus, we got our own thing goin', we don't need anybody to tell us what it's all about," and "Drop kick me, Jesus, through the goalposts of life." This is no joke; these are real country-western songs, and country-western songs are great at capturing our values in unforgettable word pictures.

If I were to say to you that apart from the church there is no salvation, you would probably think that I was Catholic. But this statement is not mine. It was spoken by many church fathers and reformers. Calvin writes in his *Institutes of Christian Religion*, "Beyond the pale of the Church no forgiveness of sins, no salvation, can be hoped for" (IV.1.4) and "those to whom he is Father, the Church may also be Mother" (IV.1.1). The Westminster Confession of Faith also states in article 25.2, "out of which (the Church) there is no ordinary possibility of salvation." The church is not an option for Christians. It is an essential, particularly if we understand the communal and external nature of our salvation. God's salvation includes our experiencing, right now in the present, being reconciled to him and others and entering the new age where we experience a foretaste of heaven in our life together—through the application of the work of Christ in each of our lives.

Not only is the church an earthly manifestation of a heavenly reality, it is the primary way or means God uses to save us. How are we saved? How are we made right with God? "By grace, through faith" would be the correct answer. But how does God give his grace to us? Theologians tell us that God communicates his grace to us through the preaching of the Word, the sacraments, and prayer—all things that are functions of the church.

At the same time, we become part of the process of sharing God's grace with others. Paul writes, "But grace was given to each one of us according to the measure of Christ's gift" (Ephesians 4:7). If I need grace to be saved, then who has my grace? *You do!* And I have the grace that you need to be saved.

The only way I can experience the fullness of God's salvation in my life is if I'm part of a community of believers who are gracing one another in their daily lives. This is exactly what the church is to be and why it is essential. We can only experience all of God's salvation together when we share his grace among us.

Western individualism has turned the church into an event that I may or may not participate in, depending on what I get out of it. This is not what the church is to be. It is a community of people who bring the best of the grace that God has given us and give it to one another. *This* is what the church is meant to be!

What Western individualism has done can be seen in the meals served to the youth group at the typical church. These were the worst meals. You either had hot dogs, sloppy joes, or pizza with stale chips left over from the last meal. To drink there was orange-looking bug juice that had a funny aftertaste. This was all served on paper plates that you had to carry with two hands because they were so thin. The goal of these meals was to feed as many people as possible with as little preparation, trouble, and expense as possible, and by as few people as possible. The result was far from something you looked forward to. Unfortunately, most of our churches spiritually look like the youth group meals, rather than the feasting table the church is meant to be.

When I was a boy, my favorite part of church was the potluck supper. I don't know if you have potluck suppers in a Presbyterian church, but we had them and I loved them. My mouth waters when I think of the favorite dishes that the women in our church were known for. Mrs. Oliver would always bring, along with other things, home-made rolls and blackberry jelly. Mrs. Williams was renowned for her coconut cake; she always used fresh coconut. Mrs. Johnson always brought the best fried chicken. My mother, like the other women, would always bring several dishes, and one of the dishes she brought was deviled eggs. Again, I don't know if you should take deviled eggs to a church dinner, but they're my favorite food.

My mother always called my sister and me to help her peel the eggs. I always asked her, "Mom, can I have a deviled egg now?" and she always answered, "No, these are for church!"

At the dinner there was always an unbelievable spread—more food than we could possibly eat. My parents must have never been too hungry because we always waited at the end of the line. Children had to stay with their parents, and the parents supervised what children put on their plates. I could never take more than two deviled eggs, but I could always go back for more if I wanted more. I just had to clean my plate first.

One Wednesday afternoon when we were making deviled eggs for the church dinner, I asked my mom, "Mom, can we make deviled eggs just for our family to eat here at home so we don't have to share them with all the people at church?"

My mother answered, smiling, "No."

"Why not?" I groaned.

My mother, who was the kindest person anyone had ever met and a wonderful mother, said matter-of-factly, "They are too much trouble."

I wondered, *If deviled eggs were too much trouble to make for your own flesh and blood, why would my mother go to all the trouble of making them for the church?* But my mother understood that the church family is where you give yourself in sacrificial service. You do more for your church family than you would even do for yourself.

The church is to be a spiritual banquet, where we all bring the grace God has given us and share it with one another. We should share that grace the same way God shared it with us. Because he has lavished his grace on us (Ephesians 1:8), we should lavish it on one another. When we do so, the church becomes a community where the promises of God are lived out among the people making the church heaven on earth.

I know that I have to be part of a community where God's promises are incarnated in the lives of its people. I wish I could say that when I read in the Bible that God loves me unconditionally that that is enough for me, but I need more. I need to be loved unconditionally by others! I wish I could say that when I am forgiven of my sin that that is enough, but I need also to experience that forgiveness by you forgiving me! We need all the truths of God lived out so that the gospel is seen, heard, and experienced—not just in an individual internal way, but in the external communal expression in the community of God's people.

This understanding of the church also changes *why* we go to church. We shouldn't go thinking, *What I am going to get out of church today?* But, *How am I going to grace my brothers and sisters this morning?* Then, when someone at the dinner table asks, "How was church?" you'd respond, "Great!" The questioner would ask, "Was it a particularly good sermon or was the music special? What was it?" You'd answer, "No, neither the music nor the sermon was particularly exceptional. What made church great was that I got to grace my friend who I found out was going through a very difficult time. You should have seen the joy that came over him! I wouldn't have missed that for the world. I can't wait to see who I'm going to grace *next week!*"

This understanding of church not only changes the way we go to church, it changes how we think about church. Church is no longer just a gathering on Sunday mornings; it becomes a nonstop community—where any day of the week or at any time, day or night, when the Lord lays a brother or sister on our heart, we grace them. This makes church a party.

Our Lord compares his kingdom and even heaven itself to a party—a feast—but we have turned that party into something not many people want to attend. This makes sharing the gospel very difficult, because most people will bring up the church as a poor example or share a negative experience they've had in the church. It is hard to invite others to a party when the people we are inviting believe that the room will be filled with a bunch of party-poopers. We have become like Jesus's description of the Pharisees: "'We played the flute for you, and you did not dance; we sang a dirge, and you did not weep'" (Luke 7:32).

Not only have our individual and internal values impacted the way we understand the gospel and the church, it also impacts the way we do evangelism. We practice "personal evangelism," "friendship evangelism," or "one-on-one evangelism." We indoctrinate our children at an early age to this individual approach. Every child who has ever attended a Vacation Bible School and sung the chorus, "I Will Make You Fishers of Men," has been taught that evangelism is something we do by ourselves.

There is nothing wrong with the words of the chorus; after all, they come straight out of the Bible. It's the choreography. We teach our children that evangelism is fishing with a pole. We make the gestures of casting a fishing rod while we are singing. However, our Lord was not speaking about fishing with a rod when he called the disciples to follow him. He was talking to fishermen who used nets. When you fish with nets, you must fish *together*.

I love fishing. I love to catch as many fish as I possibly can. I will never forget watching a *National Geographic* special on the people of the Polynesian Islands. One of the ways they caught fish was that the entire population of the island got together and made a human net across the lagoon. They lined up side by side together, holding palm branches that formed a human (palm branch) wall, while they all moved forward together. As they got closer to the shore, the fish were packed so closely together that the water was black with fish. People on the shore scooped up nets full of fish. Alone, it would be impossible to catch that many fish! But together they caught more fish than they possibly could have imagined.

The evangelism that the church is to practice should resemble the way Polynesians catch fish. We must do it together, and we do it by inviting our nonbelieving friends to the party. We let the grace that we have been lavishing on one another spill out onto the nonbelievers among us.

There is nothing wrong with personal evangelism. Philip, in Acts, was a great personal evangelist, but he is the exception and not the norm. What we have done by stressing personal evangelism is discourage more Christians from evangelizing. We have made it the "gift" of a few, rather than the practice of a community.

Philip won people to Christ, but not as many as the community of believers who were partying in Jerusalem did. Luke describes their activities: "And day by day, attending the temple together and breaking bread in their homes, they received their food with glad and generous hearts, praising God and having favor with all the people. And the Lord added to their number day by day those who were being saved" (Acts 2:46–47).

Every year in my classes I ask my students, "Who has the gift of evangelism?" In a full room, only one or two will raise their hands. The percentage is about the same in the church. People don't believe they have the gift of evangelism, so they leave that difficult job to the professionals.

Every Christian knows, or at least should know, that they have been given a gift or gifts from God. When you use your gifts to grace believers, we call that edification, but when you use your gifts to grace nonbelievers—when you pour out God's grace upon them—we call that evangelism. This is what I call party evangelism. Every one of us, then, has a part in the evangelistic mission of the church. Your job, along with other believers, is to grace the socks off the nonbelievers around you. If *I* need you to make the gospel real to me, how much more do nonbelievers around us need to see God's love and God's forgiveness being lived out in us?

I call this "the hard gospel," because it takes the words that people hear us speak and makes it impossible for nonbelievers to leave the party without bumping into incarnations of the message they've just heard. It's the hard gospel in two ways: it's hard on us because we're called to live out our faith; and it's hard for our nonbelieving friends to get over experiencing grace.

When we have people over for dinner and speak about the gospel, we hope and pray that they'll see the gospel in how we treat one another, feel the gospel in how we treat them, and hear the gospel in clear and powerful words. My wife uses her gifts of hospitality, mercy, and encouragement with our non-Christian friends; and I use my gift of evangelism. The way my wife incarnates the gospel for our guests leaves a lasting impact on them, and I hope my words point them to Christ. In party evangelism, *everyone* evangelizes, using the gifts they've been given.

Not long ago, a woman shared how many factors had influenced her to join our church and to come to Jesus. The invitation of a neighbor who was already a member of our church, the teaching she heard in the church, the love and concern she felt from others in the church as they lived out the gospel, and the practical ways she was served by the deacons—all of these things and more played a role in her coming to Christ.

Party evangelism is not only much better than personal evangelism—it's much more effective and fun. In personal evangelism, we usually feel like it's us against the world. We're dragged into a conversation about the gospel over lunch with friends or coworkers, and they all seem to jump on us. Bruised and battered, we vow to never speak up again. Party evangelism is more like tag-team wrestling. My family used to go to wrestling matches when I was a child, and they haven't changed in the fifty years I've been watching them. In a tag-team wrestling match there is always that moment where the referee is distracted by one wrestler, and the wrestler's partner is thrown into their opponent's corner. There, he is held by one man while the other beats on him unmercifully. Good thing it's staged!

In party evangelism, however, the results are the complete opposite. We outnumber nonbelievers, and instead of getting bashed they get graced, mercifully, in word and deed.

Jesus was a great party evangelist. We know this because of what his enemies said about him. They called Jesus a drunkard and glutton (Luke 7:34). All that means is that Jesus knew how to have fun at a party. Jesus knew how to grace the people at whatever table he found himself. He graced the tables of the religious and nonreligious, the righteous and the unrighteous, one as easily as the other.

If we're going to be known as a partying church and reach non-Christians, we're going to have to lower the walls that separate us from the world around us. Christians have believed that the best way to be holy is to separate themselves from the world around them. We build high walls around our churches. These are not physical walls—those would actually be easier to get around. Nonetheless, they are real barriers to keep out people we don't want at our party, people who would be a bad influence, people who don't have a proper upbringing—those who are not "our kind of people." We believe that if we keep these people out of the church, we will be a holier people. Isolation from the world is believed to be the best defense against worldliness.

The result is just the opposite of what we desire. We are different from the world around us, but not in any significant way. What we end up with is a form of religion that just covers our worldliness with a thin veneer of religiosity.

A partying church, on the other hand, has low walls. A partying church doesn't talk about how evil everyone else is, but how bad we *all* are. You don't hear the partying church talking about other peoples' sins; instead they talk about their *own* sin. And you hear the call of the gospel offered to all.

A partying church doesn't try to get all their people into the church all the time, to keep them away from all those "unholy people." Instead, they have fewer meetings and try to give their people time to get out into the world to be Christian with their family and neighbors. Partying churches don't hold exercise classes in church to be "attractional"; they go to classes in the community. They don't have everyone in a church softball league; they send their members out to join community leagues. (Some church leagues, by the way, can be so nasty that they exhibit anything but grace to one another.)

There is a risk when we send our people out into the world—that we would see the truth about ourselves. We might find out that we're more worldly than we are holy. This may actually cause us to apply the gospel to our own lives, producing humility and grace in us, making it a lot easier to extend grace to others.

Recently, a young man in our church asked me if I would pray for a friend of his that he has known for many years. His friend grew up in a Christian home; all his siblings are Christian and doing well in life. But this young man struggles with depression, alcoholism, and drugs. The young man says that he believes the facts of the gospel, who Jesus is and what he has done, but he doesn't believe that God could be gracious to him because he is so "bad." He believes he is incapable of change—and that God is incapable of changing him. He went on to say that the young man has never seen very much grace in the church. The tragedy is that his entire life he sat as a wallflower in the church and never once, according to him, got bumped by grace.

If the Christian community is going to challenge our culture, we as the church must begin by being a place where the gospel is communally lived out toward the external world. When we do this, the world around us will see the lights and hear the music. And they will repent and come to the party.

Discussion Questions

1. What blessings have you been blessed with and how can you bless others with them?

2. What are the low walls and high walls around your church? What can you do to lower the unnecessary high walls around your church?

3. What does evangelism as a community look like? How can your community group practice party evangelism?

6

Be More Than a Friend

Friendship evangelism is *not* biblical!

OK, that's an overstatement. And yet, the conventional wisdom today is that friendship evangelism is the *only* form of evangelism. We all have a story of how we led a friend to Christ, or even how we came to faith through the influence of a friend. In fact, friendship is so stressed that it would seem that "being a friend" is all that's needed to win people to Christ. It is *this* underlying belief that is so unbiblical.

Our Lord asks us to be much more than a friend to others. To love your friends doesn't take a great deal of grace, most of the time. Anyone can love their friends. Our Lord told us as much: "If you love those who love you, what benefit is that to you? For even sinners love those who love them. And if you do good to those who do good to you, what benefit is that to you? For even sinners do the same" (Luke 6:32–33).

What *does* our Lord ask us to do? He asks us to love our enemies (Luke 6:27), pray for those who persecute us (Matthew 5:44), and bless those who curse us (Luke 6:28). Fully biblical evangelism is, in fact, *enemy* evangelism—loving, blessing, and praying for our enemies. We don't need Jesus in order to love our friends—most of the time! We don't have to rely on his grace to be kind to those we care about. Therefore, the world pays no attention to our bold statements about how different Christ has made us when there's nothing extraordinary needed to love and care for our friends alone.

To love our enemies requires God to show up in our lives. To forgive those who have deeply hurt us can only be the fruit of the Holy Spirit working in our hearts. To pray for those who curse us is evidence of Christ in us. Making our enemies the object of our outreach requires us to change, because in reaching out to our enemies we become deeply aware of our own need of Christ and his grace. We realize that we need Christ as much, if not more, than our enemies do.

Enemy evangelism is dependent on Christ and the Holy Spirit. Friendship evangelism puts the focus on us, limiting the power of the gospel to our ability to be friendly. At the heart of friendship evangelism is the unspoken belief that the more people know me, the more they will want Jesus. But is that really the case? Don't we all have close friends, even family members, who have known us longer than we have been Christians—and who are no more interested in the gospel today than the first time we shared our faith with them? If friendship is the true power behind evangelism, wouldn't more of our closest friends and family come to faith as a result of our friendship?

If our close friends and family aren't becoming Christians, and we believe friendship is what empowers the gospel, shouldn't we accept the responsibility for their lack of response and ask the question, "Is it because I'm not a good enough friend or because I'm not a good enough Christian—or both—that more of my friends and family haven't come to Christ?"

God may very well use your relationships with friends and family to bring them to Christ, but the gospel isn't bound by friendship. It is just one of the means God uses to turn the gospel loose in the world.

Friendship evangelism has too narrow a focus. After all, how many friends can one have? Once you have your quota of friends, there isn't much room for anyone new in your life, and thus we pass by others because they're not the "target" of our evangelistic efforts. We can even ignore others who aren't on our list. When we worked with Muslims in France, my wife noticed that I went out of my way to be friendly with Muslims and would ignore or even be rude to the French because I was trying to reach Muslims. My excuse was that the French weren't my target.

The paradigm driving friendship evangelism gives us an excuse not to witness because if we're not a friend of the person we're exempt from speaking to them. This may explain why so few Christians witness today—because they have so few friends and the friends they have are not interested in the gospel. We need to reverse the way we do things. Instead of making friends, hoping that one day they will be interested in the gospel, we should find people who are interested in the gospel and befriend them.

Christians will ask me, "What should I do if none of my friends are interested in the gospel?" The answer I give them is, "Keep your friends; their interest in the gospel could change any day. Just make room in your life for some new friends who *are* interested in the gospel."

Better to practice evangelism that is friendly than "friendship evangelism." We know no strangers because everyone we meet is owed common courtesy and friendship. Consider the lawyer who was seeking to justify himself in Luke 10, which led to Jesus's telling of the parable of the Good Samaritan. If the lawyer had been an evangelical, his question would have been, "I know I am to share the gospel, but who is my friend?" Jesus's answer would still be the same: "Whoever you come across."

Friendship evangelism can also feel as if we're prostituting our kindness and using it to manipulate others. If we do, we are no different than some cults. People will feel used instead of cared for.

Suppose I make a new friend and we really hit it off. We hang out together a lot. He invites me over for meals, we watch football together, and we help one another out with chores and repairs around the house. After some time, when I believe the relationship is strong enough, I begin looking for an opportunity to share my faith with my new friend. Up until now, I haven't even mentioned that I'm a Christian because I didn't want to scare him off. The next time we're together I broach the subject with my friend, whom we'll call Fred.

"Fred, it has really been great getting to know you these past few weeks. It has been a lot of fun—but there is something about me that you need to know."

Fred's nodding of his head in agreement now stops, and he looks puzzled. You can tell that he is drawing conclusions about what I am about to say, and he interrupts, "Hey, maybe I should have told you, I'm not gay. I am a happy heterosexual."

"No, no!" I embarrassedly answer, "I am a Christian!"

Fred's expression changes to disappointment. I get the feeling that he would have had less trouble with my sexuality than my religion. At this point Fred begins reinterpreting the past five or six weeks in light of this new information. He becomes upset and angry because he senses that he was set up—that everything I did with him had an ulterior motive.

A real approach isn't friendship evangelism, but evangelism that *is* friendly. Your faith isn't something you hide, but it naturally spills over our lives in all kinds of ways so that others know how important our faith is to us. Evangelism that is friendly understands that there are people who have no interest in the gospel and want nothing to do with us because we are Christians. We can't control that, but we can also understand that others will be drawn to us because of our faith.

There is another dirty little secret about friendship evangelism. We pick out those we want to be friends with, and most of the time these people are fun, attractive, and well-connected—the kind of people who aren't a burden to be around. They are people who have "everything," and we're hoping that we can offer them a little more (while hoping we might get some of what they've got in the process).

We would rather not think about befriending people who, if we became their friend, would appear burdensome. I say "appear" burdensome because they usually end up being more of a blessing to us—it's counterintuitive.

There was a woman who lived in the apartment building next to ours in France who had suffered horribly as a child under the Nazis in World War II. Because of the trauma she had endured, she was a fragile and broken person. Much of the time she was functional; she had a job and could care for herself. Other times, she would just shut down. She wouldn't bathe or take care of herself. During those times this woman was hard to be around, both psychologically and physically.

My wife Christy—who loves everyone and whom everyone loves—got into a conversation with her. The woman was complaining that she had no one to help her wash her hair and bathe. Without hesitation, Christy volunteered to help bathe her and wash her hair—which hadn't been washed in months. I don't know about you, but for most of us friendship stops short of the dirty job of helping someone wash their hair and bathe.

Christ doesn't just call us to have fun hanging with the guys or the gals. Mind you, there is nothing wrong with that, and we should enjoy those times. However, Jesus calls us to take up our crosses and follow him, and that means laying down our lives daily in service to others. We are called to be more than friends; we are called to be servants.

It's true that our Lord in John 15:13–15 calls his disciples friends and no longer servants; however, he says this just after washing their feet—and as he prepares to lay down his life for them. He expects the same from us.

When we returned from the mission field we met another missionary couple who had been working in South America, and we shared what we were doing on the field. The husband said that it was hard for him to make contacts in South America so he had joined the country club and played golf to make friends. Now, that is more my idea of friendship evangelism—golf at the club, not to mention drinks afterwards! Do people in country clubs need the gospel? Sure. But we must be careful that our ministry for Christ is sacrificial, rather than self-serving.

Several years ago we moved into a home that needed a lot of work. Our next-door neighbors were a retired husband and wife. Fortunately for me, he was a handyman, and because he was retired he was always available to give advice on any project, as well as loan me the tools I needed for the job. One afternoon I went over to ask for his help, and no one was home. Later, when I saw him in the driveway, I asked where he had been. He shared that he had to take his wife to the doctor; his wife had diabetes and was going in for her regular checkup. I told him that I was sorry to hear that and that I would pray for her.

Over the months we sent meals back and forth and had them over for dinner (once our house was livable). I also did a lot of praying for them, as his wife's health seemed to be deteriorating. I not only told them I was praying for them but went over and prayed *with* them, that God would watch over them and heal her.

During lunch one day, our doorbell rang. It was our neighbor. He explained that his wife was in the hospital and asked if I would come see her. I told him that I would come that evening.

When I arrived, the room was filled with children and grandchildren. My neighbor greeted me, "John, I am so glad you came! I was supposed to have my leg amputated because the spot on my heel is infected and is spreading, but when the doctors were giving me tests for the surgery they discovered that I have a much more serious problem with my heart! Tomorrow morning I am having heart surgery. When I checked into the hospital they asked me what religion I was. I told them that was a hard question to answer. I was born an Episcopalian, raised Lutheran, and became a Catholic when I married my husband; but now I live next door to a Presbyterian minister, so I guess I'm Presbyterian. The reason I asked you to come and see me was that I wanted to ask you to do something for me."

"Sure, anything—if I can do it, I will," I answered.

"If I die tomorrow, will you perform my funeral?" she asked.

"I don't expect you to die tomorrow, but if you do there are a few things you need to know if you want me to perform your funeral," I responded. I then shared the hope Christ offers us, even in the face of death. "Do you believe that?" I asked.

"Yes, I believe that," she replied. We then prayed, entrusting my neighbor's life now, and her life to come, to the Lord. For her, I had become more than a friend or even a neighbor; I had become her pastor—the person she called when she thought she might be dying.

This is why we want to be more than a friend to people. Yes, it is nice to be invited to parties and be included in special events because people think of you as fun, but more importantly, we want people to think of us at the critical times in their lives. When they get that frightening diagnosis, we want them to call us. And we want to be the kinds of friends who will respond to that call without hesitation. When their phone rings late at night with horrible news, our number should be the first one they dial, because they know that we are much more than friends.

Discussion Questions

1. How can friendship evangelism be misleading? Share some of the roadblocks you've faced in sharing the gospel with long-term friends.

2. Why is it theologically important for us to love our enemies? How does it reflect the character of our God and the nature of the gospel? How does practicing enemy evangelism change you? What are the barriers that keep you from loving your enemies?

3. What are we to be to non-Christians if we are called to be more than a friend? What are some practical ways you can do that?

7

Evangelize Christians and
Disciple Non-Christians

Conventional wisdom would say that I have the title of this chapter backwards. You disciple Christians and evangelize non-Christians, right?

However, the conventional wisdom can lead to several unhealthy results and unintended consequences that would distort our faith. One mistake this leads to is a two-tiered understanding of Christianity. In other words, we have one message for non-Christians and another message for Christians.

I was leading a Bible study for a group of Christians who wanted to go deeper in their understanding of God's Word. We had a couple who were not Christians and knew very little about the Christian faith, but who wanted to attend our study. When I asked the group if it would be good to include this couple, several in the group objected. "We can't include them—we're studying Ephesians. We'll have to change to an evangelistic Bible study, but that won't feed us spiritually." Our group had a

two-tiered understanding of Christianity; the message of the gospel had
been separated from the message of discipleship.

When we separate evangelism from discipleship, we limit what we
say to non-Christians to a few passages in the Bible that we believe are
"for" non-Christians. Our presentation of the gospel is confined to a
handful of passages, where we use the same eight to ten verses for every
situation. But what part of God's Word is *not* good news?

This two-tiered understanding of Christianity has produced two
different types of churches. Most of us have been in both. We were led
to Christ in a church that "preached the gospel"—and *only* those parts
considered to be "the gospel." We were happy for a while in this church
because we understood that our purpose was to invite our non-Christian
friends and to be props for presenting the gospel to others. It was exciting
at first to be in a gospel-preaching church because we saw people coming to Christ, but after a while we become dissatisfied with hearing the
same gospel message over and over again. Then we discovered theology
and deep rich biblical exposition, so we left the evangelistic church for a
"Bible-teaching" church.

In a Bible-teaching church you grow tremendously in your knowledge and understanding of the Lord, but you hardly ever see anyone
come to Christ. Some Bible-teaching churches even wear their lack of
converts as a badge of honor—as an affirmation that they are preaching the "true" gospel and the entire counsel of God. If someone were
to become a Christian, the church would begin to wonder if they had
compromised the faith and been preaching "easy believism," because
evangelistic churches boast in preaching the "simple gospel."

Not only does a two-tiered understanding of Christianity create two
kinds of churches; it creates two stages of the Christian faith. We mistakenly see the Christian life like a two-stage rocket. The first stage is
grace. We're quick to offer grace to non-Christians and speak of forgiveness of sin, but once someone has embraced the gospel we move them
onto stage two, discipleship—or rather, *our* version of discipleship. This
second stage is powered by works and pietistic laws. In stage one, the

message for nonbelievers is "God loves you unconditionally, and stands ready to forgive you of all your sin." The message in stage two is, "You'd better work hard practicing spiritual disciplines and improving yourself if you want God to keep loving you." Grace gets us off the ground, but we stay in orbit by our own works.

When you live under this false understanding of Christianity, the joy that you felt when you first became a Christian disappears. Instead of rejoicing in God's love and forgiveness, you either live under the condemnation that you're not doing enough and have failed your Lord—mistakenly believing that God cannot love someone who has performed as poorly as you have—or you live a lie. The lie would be that you're performing at an acceptable level for God, or at least feel you're doing more than others, and that ought to mean *something*.

When we understand the gospel as a two-stage rocket of grace and works, we cannot help but become like the Pharisees in the New Testament. Therefore, we're not very good at evangelizing others. Our Lord described the Pharisees as those who "travel across sea and land to make a single proselyte" (Matthew 23:15). Too many of us are just like the Pharisees; we have separated the message of the Christian life into grace and law.

When we begin with grace but "perfect ourselves" with law, we become angry, judgmental, critical, and just not nice people. Angry, judgmental, and critical people don't make good evangelists. We cannot share something that we have long since forgotten. What you and I need most is the same thing our unbelieving friends need: we need grace, repentance, and faith. In other words, we need the gospel!

A real approach, therefore, is to evangelize Christians and disciple non-Christians. The reason believers need to be evangelized is that grace is so easily forgotten. The natural condition of the human heart is to take a works approach to God. When we do something really great, or when we do something really stupid (either is possible at any given moment), a default switch goes on in our hearts that resets our heart back to its pre-Christian setting of works without grace. When our heart is in a position of works and not grace, we become like the Pharisees: graceless. Not the best witness.

What you and I need most to grow as Christians is to be reminded of why we became Christians in the first place. Peter's last words to us are to "grow in the grace and knowledge of our Lord and Savior Jesus Christ. To him be the glory both now and to the day of eternity. Amen" (2 Peter 3:18). If everything we're learning does not bring us back to the foot of the cross, then we are not growing in grace and Christ is not being glorified.

Jesus himself taught us at the end of the Gospel of Luke that *every* passage of Scripture points us to who he is and what he has done. "These are my words that I spoke to you while I was still with you, that everything written about me in the Law of Moses and the Prophets and the Psalms must be fulfilled" (Luke 24:44). Therefore, every passage of the Bible is evangelistic by design because it leads us to Christ. The more we grow in Christ, the more we grow in his grace, which in turn makes us more attractive communicators of the gospel.

Is it possible to disciple nonbelievers? Think about it: When did the disciples become believers? When Peter and his coworkers left their nets and followed Christ? Was it when Peter answered our Lord's question, "Who do people say that I am?" (Mark 8:27). Someone suggested once to me that Peter became a believer *after* he denied the Lord three times. Or was it on the day of Pentecost, when the disciples were at last filled with the Holy Spirit?

We need to change our vocabulary when we describe a Christian. Jesus didn't command us to go out and make *believers*, he commissioned us to go and make *disciples*. We need to move away from a "big decision" definition because all the emphasis is on making the decision, praying the prayer, or walking down the aisle. Is that all Christ asks of us?

Once we've made the "big decision" and gotten it over with, we can go on with our lives. Western evangelicalism has infected the world with this heresy—that if you have made the "big decision" you're OK; everything between you and God is fine.

In a discipleship approach, the moment of decision is played down. A decision to follow Christ is celebrated as a first step. Just like with our children, when they took that first step we applauded them—but their training wasn't over; it was just beginning. One difference between a convert-making approach and a discipleship-making approach is that the convert-making method takes a brief time. You can make a convert in a few minutes. It takes a lifetime to make a disciple.

Another difference is that a disciple-making approach changes the message we communicate to non-Christians. One of the problems of traditional evangelism is that we believe we have to keep repeating the gospel message over and over again, until our non-Christians friends believe it. If they don't believe it, we give up after repeating the same message fifty times because we know they know everything we have to say about becoming a Christian.

I remember fishing with my best friend, and I once again was sharing the gospel with him. He rolled his eyes and said to me, "Do you think I'm stupid? Do you think I *haven't* been listening? I'm tired of hearing it." The rest of the trip, we had nothing to say.

If you confine the gospel to the handful of verses that are used in gospel presentations, you will quickly exhaust what you have to say to non-Christians. But if you take a discipleship approach, the entire Bible is—all of a sudden—*useful*. It's strange that we would ever think that only certain parts of God's Word are appropriate for evangelism. Just think of the possibilities of using Ecclesiastes, Song of Solomon, or even Leviticus to share our faith!

Traditional evangelism usually only explains one doctrine—the doctrine of justification by faith. This doctrine is critical, but so much more needs to be understood. A generation ago this approach was sufficient because most people had a Christian understanding of the world, God, and themselves. Now we live in a society where we must lay those foundations again—not by continually speaking to nonbelievers about the doctrine of justification by faith, but by laying out a biblical understanding of God, this world, mankind, and how God calls us to live in the world. If our standard is having a biblical view of God, this world, mankind, and how we should live, then *all* of us need to be converted— to be transformed by the renewing of our minds (Romans 12:2)—and that is exactly my point when I speak of evangelizing Christians.

An approach that evangelizes Christians and disciples non-Christians changes the way we read the Bible. I can read Scripture in such a way that I am affirmed in my beliefs and actions, or I can read it the way it is intended to be read—as a challenge to entrust myself more to our Lord and his grace. When I read the Scripture this way I am no longer telling other people what they need to do, but instead I invite them to join me in asking for grace, repentance, and faith because we both—believers and nonbelievers—need the gospel.

How do you disciple non-Christians? *By using every circumstance and question in their lives as a window into what it means to follow Christ.* We change the focus of the message from "How do I go to heaven when I die?" to "How can heaven be brought down to earth through living in a right relationship with our heavenly Father and others?" The answer to both questions, however, is the same—through the work of Christ on the cross.

Let's return to our earlier Bible study group. We did eventually agree to let non-Christians attend, and once we saw how well the meetings were going, we made it a practice that as soon as someone became a Christian, they would not only share their testimony immediately with the group but would lead the Bible study the following week. Every time I share this story with my seminary students, there is an outcry against letting a new believer teach. In a traditional evangelism paradigm, they would be correct; new believers should not teach. But since we were already discipling nonbelievers, these new Christians were actually old disciples. They had been discipled for as long as a year and a half before they came to faith and were asked to teach.

In addition, we didn't just ask them to teach without any help; the appropriate older and more spiritually mature believers spent time helping the new converts to prepare to lead the study (another important step in the Christian life). What this teaches the new convert is that it is normal for every follower of Christ to testify and teach. Imagine how different the church and the world would be if everyone in the church was able to teach and testify.

Since that very positive experience of letting non-Christians into our Bible study group, we have gone a step further. There was a young Hindu lady, married to a believer, who was in another group we were leading. Since all the other people in this community group were mature believers, and she has never expressed any hostile attitudes towards Christianity, I asked her if she would teach the Bible study. The passage she was to prepare was James 4; her husband, the son of a Baptist minister, was available to help her prepare the study.

The next week, when she led the discussion on James 4, she did a good job of explaining (from a non-Christian's understanding) what James was saying. It was clear that she did not understand the gospel, but that week she had to wrestle with what the Bible was saying and then share what she had learned with others.

A couple of months later she gave her life to Christ. I asked her to share her testimony with the church. I was wondering if her testimony would be a murky, unclear story. What I heard shocked me. Here it is:

> It's been little over a month since I became a Christian, and the following is an account of how I got here:
>
> I was born and raised in India in a Hindu household. For those of you unfamiliar with the country, the majority of India's population is Hindu with Christians, Muslims, Sikhs, Buddhists, and people of other faiths making up the minority. Growing up, I was never particularly religious and my parents never really "pushed" religion onto us. Apart from occasional visits to the temple and certain prayers offered during various religious festivals I would say my spiritual life was pretty nonexistent. Hinduism as a religion is very hard to define. The lines between religious belief, social custom, and cultural

norms are often blurred. It is hard for me to sum up for you in one line what Hinduism is all about or what it means to be a Hindu. I did not believe in reincarnation and always thought that once I was dead that was it, nor did I understand what possible good could come from a priest reciting prayers for me in Sanskrit, a language as alien to me as Latin is to most people today. It always felt like I was just born a Hindu and whether I chose to practice the religion or not, or believed in any aspect of it or not, I would always remain one.

Ironically enough, I received my formative education in institutions established and run by the Catholic Church. The majority of the population in these schools remained Hindu. Every morning we would assemble for fifteen minutes of prayer time and I guess everyone would pray according to whatever religious beliefs they held. But we would also recite The Lord's Prayer. Now with the exception of the few Christians amongst us, I would guess none of us knew that these were the very words of Christ. And I suppose because the prayer did not specifically have the words "Jesus" or "Christ" in it, it was considered secular enough to recite without hurting anyone's religious sensibilities. It is only recently that I have come to understand what it means to recite this particular prayer. So having been educated in this manner and at different times having been part of nativity plays and Christmas celebrations, I have always known about Jesus. But there is a world of difference in knowing about Jesus and having a personal relationship with him.

Anyway, life continued on. If you are expecting a hard luck story because I grew up in a poor, developing country, there isn't one. In many ways I would say I led a charmed life. I would even describe it as a life of immense privilege. Although we weren't exactly wealthy, we were relatively well off and I certainly didn't want for anything. In middle class India, education is everything and all I was expected to do was excel at school and not do anything to dishonor the family name. My early twenties were spent attending college and then pursuing a professional degree. That done, it was on to getting a job, which I did. Since I was single and had not yet met anyone that I cared enough to marry, the next step was an arranged marriage. It was at that point in my life, eight years ago, that I met Tim, and life has never been the same. In retrospect I suppose I was living God's plan all along even if I didn't know it at the time. One could argue that the decisions we had both made in our lives regarding our education, careers, where we chose to live, etc., had led us to the point where we were both attending a conference in Delhi at the same time.

But if you really think about it, so many things would have had to fall into place from the moment we were born to the moment we met. What were the chances that two people who lived such disparate lives could possibly meet, fall in love, and get married? This was the work of a Divine Hand. The decision to get married was not an easy sell to either of our families. My family was not thrilled at the idea of having an American for a son-in-law, convinced as they were that all Americans lived rather amoral lives and Tim's character could be no different. They revised their opinion after their first meeting with Tim. For Tim's side of the family the objection remained the religious difference. Despite it all, I moved to Philadelphia six years ago and we got married.

Now I had to adjust not only to married life, but to life here in the US as well. To say it was a challenge would be putting it mildly. We were living in Center City, a block away from Tenth Presbyterian Church, and started attending services there. This was my first real introduction to the gospel and I have to say I wasn't a big fan. I enjoyed the music and loved it when the Westminster Brass played but I didn't care to be told every Sunday that I was a sinner. I knew I wasn't perfect and yes, I had a few faults, but then who doesn't? I considered myself a good person and had led, what I believed, a more or less morally upright life. I didn't think there was anything wrong with the way I was living my life. And so I continued to attend church in this ambivalent way for more than a year: Hearing the Word of God but not really listening to what it said to me. By this time we had started looking for a house and had decided to confine our search to the Mt. Airy section of Philly. We loved the neighborhood and its proximity to Center City and it was as suburban a life as I could imagine myself living.

And then one Sunday we heard John Leonard speak at Tenth Presbyterian about a church plant they were considering in the Mt. Airy/Chestnut Hill area. After the service we went up to John and Christy and introduced ourselves, and once again life was going to change in ways I could not have foreseen. Well, we bought our house in Mt. Airy and John visited us a few times as we settled in. And then we attended the first service of Cresheim Valley Church at the Masonic Lodge. Over the next few months we got to know the small congregation. For Tim, it felt like he had finally found a church he wanted to be a part of, and for me, it felt like I had, in part, found the family I had so missed since moving to this country. With my family in India and Tim's scattered around the country, it was wonderful to be embraced by John and Christy and the entire congregation. This was four years ago and I count many close friends here today.

I now wonder why I didn't become a Christian at that time. I guess I still wasn't ready to fully accept what the gospel was saying to me, although perhaps now I was keeping an open mind about it. And so in these last few years I have listened, be it in church on Sunday mornings or on Wednesday nights during Bible study. As I had questions, Tim answered them for me as best as he could. And increasingly so did our Bible study group, no matter how basic the question or even how silly. And yet I was not prepared to commit my life to Christ. At one point I felt like I had to study Hinduism and really try and figure it out before I could decide whether I wanted any part of it or not. And then part of me felt like I would be betraying my heritage by turning my back on Hinduism. For someone who has been raised on a steady diet of Indian mythology and historical fact dating back 5,000 years it all seemed too fantastic to believe that 2,000 years ago God sent his only Son to walk amongst men and by his sacrifice save us all. But perhaps in the end my biggest struggle was accepting that I could be saved by his grace alone; that in this instance I couldn't earn my way and my actions would not ensure that I would receive his grace.

I also knew by this time that I was at a crossroads in life, an awareness that something was missing—a feeling that I needed to make some kind of decision. Well, the last few months have been difficult. I quit my job to stay home with the children and have been looking for ways to preserve my sanity through these long winter months. With Tim's busy work schedule, most days I have had to deal with a hyperactive toddler and the demands of a newborn pretty much on my own. I was short on patience and ill-tempered and worried about all manner of things to the point where I could not sleep at night. Finally one night, as I lay in bed with a million thoughts running through my head and facing the prospect of another restless night I decided to pray. I prayed to Jesus to ease my worries, to come into my heart, and basically "take over me." At some point I must have dozed off. I woke up a couple of times after that and each time I woke up I felt calm and rested. Eventually I slept through the rest of the night and when I woke up in the morning I felt very much at peace. I just felt different. I am amazed by how palpable the change is. It seemed as though Christ had been by my bedside all night and tended to me much as a parent would tend to a sick child. And so began my new life—a Christian life. All the reasons I held earlier for not converting seemed inconsequential. In the end it all seemed so clear and simple.

Well, life is good. Tim and I have no reason to complain. We have been blessed with a lot, not the least of which are two wonderful sons. And I know nothing would make us happier than to have them grow up into Christian men. I know that there will be difficult times in our lives. There will be moments when I shall feel completely helpless. I will worry about things I cannot change or control. But I am no longer alone. He is always with me. He will never forsake me. And I derive great comfort from that.

I had mentioned earlier that I could not describe Hinduism or what it meant to be Hindu. But if someone were to ask me, someone unfamiliar with the gospel, what Christianity means or what it means to be a Christian I would direct them to John 14:6, "I am the Way, the Truth and the Life. No one comes to the Father except through Me." Or John 3:16, "For God so loved the world that he gave his one and only Son, that whoever believes in him shall not perish but have eternal life." What an incredible promise! I am in awe of it and humbled by His sacrifice for me. (Used by permission.)

If you find it hard to believe that a new Christian could do such a good job of articulating her faith, just remember that this woman was discipled for four years before she converted.

We must evangelize Christians, and disciple non-Christians!

Discussion Questions

1. How might you encourage one another in the gospel right now in your community?

2. How would a discipleship approach to evangelism change how you are interacting with people about the message and the method of the gospel?

3. Discuss some of the ways we are the barriers to people coming to Christ when they attend our Bible studies. What can we do to make them feel more welcomed and understood?

8

Let Christ Lead People to You

In traditional evangelism, the emphasis is on leading people to Christ. Our Lord commands us to share our faith, and the Bible teaches that believers play an indispensable role in that process. However, we can overemphasize our role in evangelism so much so that we forget the larger, more fundamental work of God. It is the Holy Spirit, working in the hearts of non-Christians in many ways, who opens their eyes and softens their hearts.

God may choose to use us to be a part of that process, but our role is always secondary and God's role primary. When we make our role primary and God's role secondary, our prayers are also affected. Prayer is treated as less important as we spend most of the time in planning, strategizing, and marketing.

It's important to plan and strategize, but we live in an age where we put far too much importance on what we do and how we do it than calling on God in prayer to do *his* work. In addition, prayer gives us the right perspective on who we are and what our role is in evangelism. Often, prayer will bring about more change in us than the people for whom we are praying. Why should we tell others to depend on and trust in Christ when we don't demonstrate that we depend on and trust Christ in the way we share our faith?

When God's role is primary we reverse the roles of planning and prayer. Instead of opening and closing our planning meeting in short perfunctory prayers, we spend the time that we used to spend in planning praying, and the time we use to spend praying, planning. This strikes the right balance and shows people that we actually believe what we're saying.

On the other hand, when we consider our work primary and God's secondary we're tempted to change the message so it becomes more palatable and our initial response rate to the gospel is improved. We stop talking about sin and repentance, instead emphasizing only love and grace. We avoid God's holiness and wrath, speaking only of his patience and kindness. The result may not be true conversion, but rather giving people a false assurance.

An overemphasis on our importance not only affects the content of the gospel we present; it can also affect the way we present it. The belief that it is up to us to lead people to Christ can cause us to be overzealous— speaking more than we should and sharing the gospel with people who aren't ready to receive it.

Jesus commanded us to preach the gospel to all nations (Matthew 24:14), but that teaching must be tempered with Jesus's teaching that we should not witness to everyone. He says, "Do not give dogs what is holy, and do not throw your pearls before pigs, lest they trample them underfoot and turn to attack you" (Matthew 7:6). Yet we believe that because Jesus commanded us to preach the gospel we have to speak to everyone— and to keep talking until they believe.

We should learn from the Jehovah's Witnesses and the Mormons, because when you tell them you're busy and can't speak to them, most of them politely say, "Thank you, we are sorry to bother you." After all, our Lord says, "If anyone will not receive you or listen to your words, shake off the dust from your feet when you leave that house or town" (Matthew 10:14). The Jehovah's Witnesses and Mormons are not sharing their teachings with everyone; they are looking for those who are interested in what they have to say. In fact, Luke tells us in Acts 16:6 that the Holy Spirit forbade Paul and his missionary team to preach the gospel in Asia!

Instead of trying to lead people to Christ, let Christ lead people to you. You do this by only sharing the gospel with those who are truly interested in hearing it.

I learned this while working with Muslims in France. Many Muslims wanted to talk about Christianity and Islam, but it wasn't because they were interested in the gospel; they were interested in disproving Christianity and converting *me*. Too often, these conversations were just arguments about what Muslims believe and what Christians believe. All my convincing arguments never led one Muslim to Christ.

But I noticed that there *were* Muslims who were coming to faith. These Muslims, for many reasons, wanted to know about Christianity because they were interested in the gospel. You had to answer the same questions, but the attitude was completely different. They wanted to learn, whereas the others just wanted to argue.

My friend, who is an expert fly fisherman, compares witnessing to fly-fishing for trout. When you're wading and see a trout, you want to present the fly in as natural a way as possible. If the trout doesn't take the bait you might try again, but to keep thrashing the water with your fly if the trout doesn't bite is no way to catch trout. Leave that fish, and find another one that may be interested! You can always come back later, and maybe then you'll find a hungry trout.

Most of the people Jesus taught found him. How do people find you? Ask your heavenly Father to send them, and keep your eyes out for everyone who comes along as the possible answer to your prayers.

Our Lord still leads us the same way that he led Philip to the Ethiopian eunuch in Acts 8. Philip met the eunuch as he rode in his chariot, reading Isaiah. God is still working in the hearts of many people. They read his Word and they don't understand it. They are looking for someone like us to explain it to them. The people we are speaking to are the answers to our prayer—and we are the answer to the seekers' prayers because we can point them to Christ.

I had an aisle seat on a plane. When I got to my seat there were two ladies in the seats next to me. I sat down and greeted them. The lady next to me introduced herself and her seat partner. After I introduced myself, the woman asked me what I did. I told her I was a pastor. She was shocked and said, "You're not going to believe this, but the woman next to me and I have been having a conversation about Christianity since we checked in. I had just told her that if a pastor sits down beside us, then I know the Lord is trying to tell me something." We spent the rest of the flight talking and reading the Scriptures together. By letting everyone know that you are a believer, people will either automatically withdraw *from* you or be drawn *to* you.

Letting Christ bring people to you means never saying more than people want to hear. There are many times I have begun to share my faith with someone, and discovered not long into that conversation that the person isn't interested. Why do we feel if we keep talking we can change their minds? It is God that changes hearts, not my words. God may use your words, but if people are not interested in what you have to say, stop talking. The gospel is a precious gift and should only be given to those who deeply desire it.

And again, the way we often discover those who deeply desire the gospel—and for that matter, how *they* find *us*—is through prayer. Through prayer, God prepares both us and those with whom we share Christ for the right encounter at the right time.

I learned this lesson during our first term in France. Our first year on the mission field in France was a very difficult year so we decided to go home for vacation in August. Our decision was confirmed when we learned that it would be cheaper to fly home than to vacation in France. We would also be able to visit our families and rest from an emotionally, spiritually, and psychologically devastating year.

I called our home church and told them we would be there in August, and they asked me to preach while the pastor was away the first two Sundays of the month. The first Sunday went really well; it was wonderful to see our friends. A close friend, Valerie, came up and said to Christy and me, "John, if you stay and be our pastor we'll bring the Muslims to you!" I laughed to myself, thinking, *She has no idea how difficult reaching Muslims is. It's naïve to think they are so easy to convert.*

The next Sunday was a special day. I conducted a baptism, and then we were invited to eat lunch with the family. A long line of people formed after church, waiting to speak with us. After many hugs and goodbyes, when there were only a few people left in line, one of the elders came up beside me and asked if he could speak to me for a moment. He had a concerned look. After excusing myself, I stepped aside to talk to him.

"John," he said, "There's a Latino man in the parking lot who says he has something to confess and would like to speak to the Father. I told him we're not a Catholic church and that he could speak to me and I would be glad to hear what he had to say, but he insisted he has to speak to the Father."

I sighed and asked, "Did he give you any indication what he has to confess? You know, this is our last day here and we leave for France tomorrow. The family whose son we just baptized has asked us over for a special lunch and they are waiting for us. Can't you speak to him?"

"I tried to get him to speak with me but he insisted on speaking with the Father," the elder said.

"But what does he want? What if he has murdered someone? What should I do? What if he's a drug dealer—after all, this is Dade County, Florida. Who knows what this guy has to confess? I really don't know how I can be of any help to him, leaving tomorrow for France." I was looking for any reason to get out of what seemed to be an unpleasant situation.

"He's waiting in the parking lot. What should I tell him?" the elder asked.

It's not often people show up at church with something to confess, so I thought I should at least take the time to meet our Latino confessor and see what he had to say. I looked over at my wife. She had already decided what I should do and said, "I'll take the kids over to lunch; you get there when you can!" I kissed her on the cheek, thanked her, and said, "This shouldn't take long."

"Sure," she said, "I'll see you when I see you. Be careful!"

The parking lot was on the other side of the church building. I walked through the hallway and out into the parking lot where the elder had said the Latino man was waiting. He was easy to find because the parking lot was empty and he was parked at the far end, in the last parking space. His old white Toyota was still running. I wondered if this was a drive-by shooting with a man who had some type of vendetta against priests. The Domino's Pizza sign in the back seat made the whole thing seem even stranger.

When he saw me coming across the lot, he got out of his car and stood beside it. He was of medium height, slim, with dark curly hair, and wearing a white T-shirt, blue jeans, and sneakers. His tanned complexion and Latino look was common in South Florida.

When I got within a few yards of him, I reached out my hand and said, "Hi, I'm the pastor of the church. How can I help you?"

The young man stepped toward me to shake my hand, "My name is Farid," he said with an Arabic accent. "I'm a Palestinian from Bethlehem. I'm here today because I want to confess Jesus as my Lord, and I want to become a Christian."

At that moment I thought about what Valerie had said a week earlier, "We'll bring the Muslims to you!" This had to be a joke someone was playing on me, and I looked around, believing I had been set up. But there was only the two of us—Farid and me.

I asked him, "Why do you want to become a Christian, and why did you decide to come to this church today?"

Farid began to recount his story.

I was born in Bethlehem into an important Muslim family, but I never felt that Islam was for me. I never practiced Islam, except for keeping the fast at Ramadan, but everyone fasts during Ramadan. When I was in high school, each day I walked by the church where Jesus was born. Beside the church there was a beautiful garden that seemed calm and peaceful. One day I decided to go inside and sit in that quiet place. I liked the garden so whenever I had time on my way home from school I would go sit in it. That garden became a special place for me.

One day, while I was enjoying the garden, one of the Fathers asked if he could sit next to me. He said he had often seen me in the garden. I told him I hoped I was allowed to be there since I was a Muslim. The Father was very nice and said, "I'm happy that you are enjoying the garden; please feel free to come back whenever you like." Over the next several years, the Father and I became friends. We spoke about many things, but what I enjoyed most was listening to stories about Jesus.

As Muslims we're taught to honor Jesus as a prophet, and although there's a chapter in the Qur'an that speaks about Jesus, we don't know a lot about him. I had never known any of the stories the Father told me. The more we spoke together the more I began to believe that Jesus was the truth and that I must follow him, but I was afraid to convert to Christianity because of my family. So I kept all of these things a secret. No one knew about the time I spent in the garden or about the conversations I had with the Father.

I decided I would come to America to do my university studies and that while I was here I would confess my faith in Jesus.

I was still cautious. In my conversations with Muslims I had learned that many times the true reason behind someone's interest in Christianity was not a legitimate motive for becoming a Christian. The most common requests were for a wife or for a visa to come to America, and many believed that because you're an American you can get them into the country. But Farid's story seemed genuine, and he was already in the States. "So how did you choose to come to this church on this Sunday?" I asked.

"Well," Farid began, "when I was delivering pizzas for Domino's last night I drove down this street and God told me to come to this church to make my confession."

I was shocked. We are not the only church on that road, and had Farid gone to any of the other churches it would have been unlikely that he would have found someone who could help him, but the Lord sent him to the church where I "happened" to be speaking.

"And why is the car running?" I asked.

Laughing, Farid answered, "I have a dead battery, so I leave the car running."

I told Farid that we had a lot to talk about and asked him if he would mind going to a friend's home with me where we could speak. He agreed, and after calling my friend to make sure he was home and that I could come by, Farid and I drove there together. Because I was leaving for France the next day, I knew it was important for someone to be around to hear Farid's story and confession so that he might be guided in his new life with Christ.

We sat in my friend's living room and went over the gospel with Farid. We read the Bible and spoke together about what sin is and the effect it has on our lives, how it touches every part of us and separates us from God. We read a Scripture passage about God's righteousness and how sin can only be forgiven if it is paid for by a sacrifice of blood. We told him Jesus Christ was the Lamb of God given by our Lord to pay for our sins, which he did on the cross by dying in our place. I explained that Jesus was not just a prophet who came to tell us what God's will for our life is, but a Savior who came to save us from a life that was under God's curse and give us a new life that is under God's blessings, because we have placed our faith in Christ. We then talked about faith and how one welcomes Jesus into his life as Lord and follows him. We spoke about repentance, and that the greatest act of repentance is turning from a life of trusting and looking to ourselves to make ourselves right with God to trusting in the work of Jesus—not just to pay for our sins but to give us his Holy Spirit so that we can have the power of God to live differently.

Farid understood everything. He only asked a few questions for clarification. How different this conversation was from the ones I had with Muslims in France! There were no arguments about the Trinity. There was no doubting the Bible, no problems with the deity of Christ, his crucifixion, death, and resurrection. He had been well taught through the Bible stories the Father told to him.

I then asked Farid if he would like to become a follower of Jesus. Pausing, he smiled and said, "That is what I have always wanted."

We knelt together beside the couch. Farid prayed, "Jesus, you know I have wanted to follow you from the time I visited your church in Bethlehem. Thank you for these new friends who have explained to me how I can belong to you. I know I have sinned against you and I confess all these sins to you now. Thank you, Jesus for dying on the cross for my sins and sending your Holy Spirit to make me a different person. I now ask you to come into my life and make me yours. Help me to follow you always. Amen."

My friend and I both prayed for Farid, asking God to help him with the trials and difficulties that were ahead of him. We asked God to strengthen his faith, to help him be a witness to his family and friends, and to protect him from doubt.

After praying, we stood and hugged one another. Farid kept thanking us for helping him become a Christian. "Father John," he said, "I am so grateful the Lord led me to you so I could make my confession."

Look for Christ to lead people to us. Pray for it. By the way, over the years Farid and I have continued to speak on the phone, by e-mail, and even visit in person. And to this day, he still calls me Father John.

Discussion Questions

1. What are ways you have seen the gospel distorted when the emphasis is placed on getting people to respond to the gospel?

2. Where is your church in reaching others? Is the emphasis on God's leading or your strategy? What is a proper balance?

3. Have you ever been guilty of saying more than people wanted to hear? What did you do when you realized it?

9

Listen More Than You Speak

It has happened to every one of us. The conversation will turn to religion over lunch with a friend or with a group of coworkers during a coffee break. We want to say something, we want to witness, but nothing comes out of our mouths. Our Lord's words ring in our ears, "Whoever denies me before men, I also will deny before my Father who is in heaven" (Matthew 10:33). But there seems to be something more powerful than guilt at work in our lives—it is the fear of not knowing what to say. So we sit sheepishly with our heads hung, sensing how Peter must have felt when he denied our Lord three times.

Traditional evangelism only takes place when we drive home our point over and over again—when we do all the talking. We have gotten the impression that on every page of the New Testament we are commanded to preach the gospel. We know what preaching looks like because we see it in church. The model for traditional evangelism looks a lot like what preachers do on Sunday mornings. Linking evangelism to preaching in our minds raises the bar so high that most of us feel unable to do it. How can we talk intelligently for thirty minutes on *any* subject, much less the Bible?

We don't share our faith because we feel unqualified to preach *and* because preaching is seen negatively in our culture. We have all said, "Don't preach at me!" or "Preach to yourself!" The one-way communication style of preaching doesn't communicate that you care much about the person that you're speaking to. Instead, this style is associated with a holier-than-thou attitude. When we preach, the ones we are speaking to can feel that we're speaking down to them. We have the truth, and we are letting them have it.

A one-way communication style puts us in the position of power; the truth is on our side. Our victim is in the position of weakness and cowers under us. Our position is comfortable; the listener, on the other hand, is shoved down into a position of weakness. What do you do when you're in a position of weakness or feel attacked? What is your natural response? You cover up and protect yourself. This is our reflex response to any threat.

When a professional prizefighter is hurt or in the ring with a better fighter, he will cover up and protect himself from his opponent. The aging Muhammad Ali, when he fought George Foreman in the fight known as the Rumble in the Jungle, spent most of the fight covering up, grabbing hold, or running from Foreman—a tactic that would be forever remembered as the "Rope-a-Dope." The blows Foreman landed were ineffective. All Foreman was doing was tiring himself because he couldn't land any effective punches on his opponent. Eventually Ali was able to knock out Foreman, as a result of protecting himself round after round.

Adopting a preaching style will elicit any of three responses when people feel attacked: they will cover up, grab hold, or run. These responses increase geometrically the closer the person is to you. On the other hand, by listening more than you speak, you place yourself in the position of weakness and allow the person you're speaking with to have the position of power.

Why would we want to place ourselves in a position of weakness? Because the Scriptures tell us that God gives grace to the humble, and there is no better way of humbling yourself than offering to others the place of power or the place of honor. When we humble ourselves, we're not just *talking* about grace—God fills us with his grace so that those with whom we speak hear it *and* experience it. They experience the grace of God not just in words, but in the way we communicate the gospel and in the way we treat them. What better way to witness than when our message, method, and life all communicate the grace of God in Jesus Christ?

Offering the place of power to others puts them at ease. They don't feel threatened. Instead of covering up and moving away, they may even move toward you with greater openness as you communicate empathy and compassion.

In traditional evangelism we look for someone to share the gospel with. A better approach is not to go looking for people to *talk* to, but to look for people to *listen* to.

On the first day of my evangelism course at seminary, the students arrive, open their laptops, and sit ready to listen intently and diligently take notes. But taking notes isn't what happens in my class. When I arrive I tell them to put away their laptops, pack up their bags, and prepare to go with me out onto the street. It is time for on-the-job training.

Once we're on the street, I like to watch the students. Most of them spend their time walking around, looking for someone to talk to. It isn't that no one is on the street; the street is filled with people. What they're looking for is the right type of person to evangelize—someone who, because of his personal demeanor, communicates, "Talk to me; I am friendly and open to speaking to you." What usually happens is that the young strong men who are ready to take on the world with nothing but the gospel of Christ will bypass big burly men and gravitate toward little old ladies.

We are not ashamed of the gospel of Christ—just scared to death to share it. We must reverse that process. We need to present ourselves in such a way that people feel comfortable approaching us and speaking to us. My wife Christy has this gift. She will come home from the grocery store and ask, "Do I have a sign on my forehead that says, 'Please speak to me?'" She then describes all the people who walked up to her and started a conversation, or who asked her a question.

When I go to the grocery store no one talks to me. You want to know why? I am on a mission. When I go shopping, it is to get in and get out of there as fast as I can. The sign I wear on my forehead is not, "Please talk to me because I'm open and interested in talking to you." Rather it's, "I'm not interested; leave me alone." Not only do people avoid speaking to me—they move out of the way when they see me coming.

Too many of us wear signs on our foreheads that read, "I'm not interested; leave me alone," or "I haven't got any time for you" as we pass by hundreds of people every day—some of whom are desperately looking for someone who will listen to them.

Christy also notices how few people really listen. We will come home from a party and she will say, "So and so talked my ear off and didn't ask one question about me or my family." Most people are willing to talk about themselves nonstop, but few want to listen. A good listener is a rare commodity—so rare that we're willing to pay large sums of money for just an hour of their time.

I was headed to the West Coast to teach and booked a late flight. The gate agent began an announcement that I believed was the boarding call for my flight, but instead was what every traveler fears: the flight was being canceled due to a mechanical problem. There were groans from the passengers. The gate agent informed us there was room on the next flight at the gate across the concourse. Before she could finish, there was a stampede to the gate, and a long line formed to rebook our seats.

I took my place in line behind a young man who looked to be in his early thirties. As we waited the young man turned to me, commenting, "This is the last thing I needed!" Since he had taken the initiative to speak to me, I asked him, "Are you leaving home, or headed home?" He turned to answer me and I noticed the hurt in his eyes. I had assumed that the emptiness in his eyes was just tiredness but I could see there was pain. He said, "I am headed home."

"What brought you to Philly?" I asked. The young man paused, and looking down he said, "My brother was in a car accident and is on life support in the hospital. My mother and I have to decide in the next couple of days if we should turn off the life support."

What makes an absolute stranger a confidant? It happens when you're desperate for someone to speak to, and no one else is available. These are not rare occurrences, if we're willing to listen more than we speak. I had a neighbor who hardly ever spoke to me, but one day he had to talk to me because he needed to confess that he'd had an affair. Once on the streets of Philly, a young man told me that he was coming from his brother's funeral. There have been parents who have spoken to me about their children, and children that wanted to talk about their parents. There are always wives or husbands who want someone to talk to about their marriage—all strangers who need someone to listen.

You will not believe how many people will want to talk to you— if you'll only take off the sign that reads "Not interested; leave me alone." You will not have to go looking for people; they will find you. There will be many people who "just happen" to be in front of you or behind you in a line. They may be strangers standing beside you at a bus stop, or in front of you at the deli counter. They may ask you, "How's the pastrami?" but what they're really asking is, "Do you care enough about me to listen?" They are desperate to talk to someone. They may believe that no one cares, that no one wants to hear their story. They can't think of any reason to live, or wonder if anyone would care if they chose to end their life. When they look at us, what will they see—the sign that says "I'm not interested; leave me alone," or the one that reads, "I care; I'll listen"?

All it takes to let others know we care is to say, "Hi, how are you doing today?" If we say it in such a way that the person we're addressing knows we have the time and are willing to listen to an answer longer than "fine," we might discover that our lives will begin to resemble the life of our Lord—where our day, like his day, was constantly being interrupted by people who had to speak to him.

We listen more than we speak not only to communicate real care and concern, but because listening will help us know what the Lord wants us to say to the person that he has brought across our path. In traditional evangelism you already know what you're going to say. You've memorized an outline of the gospel with Bible verses and illustrations that go along with each point, and you use this presentation regardless of the person and the particular need he may have. You've got one tool in the toolbox—a hammer—and you're determined to use it. I recommend that every Christian learn three or four different presentations of the gospel because there will be times when those presentations *should* be used. And yet, there is a better way.

The gospel begins with the person you're speaking to. We must listen more than we speak so that we might fully understand the person God has brought into our lives. As they speak about the immediate problems they're facing or questions they have, we should be listening and praying, asking our Lord to help us gather together everything we have heard, read, or understand from the Scriptures in order to respond to their problems or questions. Our entire response should be based on the information that we have heard from the people we're listening to.

In the West, we put far too much emphasis on the power of speaking, while overlooking the power of listening. I learned this lesson on a cruise my wife and I took for our third wedding anniversary. We arrived late to the boat and barely had time to put our luggage in our cabin and get on deck. We sat together by the pool, waiting for the castoff. The conga line was just beginning to form when a woman sat down beside us and struck up a conversation. She sat down next to my wife because she saw the sign on her forehead, "I'm friendly and happy to talk." She obviously didn't see *my* sign, "Leave us alone—we are on our anniversary!"

When my wife introduced me as a pastor, I quickly had to change my sign to "I care." We told her we were on our third anniversary, and that was the green light for her to begin sharing the long and tragic story of her own marriage. She was filled with regrets over her failed marriage because she considered herself a Christian.

She would tell us part of her story, ask a question, and before we could respond, she would answer her own question with what she already knew from the Bible. She did a pretty good job of explaining to herself what she needed to do. Just before we got into international waters and they opened up the slot machines, she had recommitted her life to Christ. We had barely said a word. Her conversations reminded me of the Psalms, where David would bring his complaint or doubt before God, and then in the second part of the psalm remind himself of the truths he knows about God and the promises God had made, and conclude the psalm by reaffirming his faith in God.

We prayed for our new friend. She was so thankful and appreciative that for the rest of the cruise, she kept introducing us as the couple who gave her so much insight into her life. My wife and I have never spent so much time listening to so many different people, sharing their heartaches and hurts, and having the opportunity to share the hope of the gospel, than we did on that cruise. That was the first and last cruise we've been on.

It is particularly important to listen when someone attacks our faith. Many times their attacks are nothing more than frustration and anger. They may only be crying out to see if anyone is listening. Nowhere are we better representatives for God than when we make it safe for others to bring their broken hearts and shattered dreams to us. It isn't so much what we tell them—it's about their discovering that God, like his people, is willing to listen and comfort those who mourn, even when the mourning is expressed in a hostile fashion.

I was having dinner in a restaurant with a few of my fellow professors when the waitress overheard our conversation. She interrupted and asked what we did. We told her we were theologians. "If God exists, I hate him," she said. Instead of looking shocked I responded, "Why don't you tell me about your god because I would probably hate him too." She began to tell us her story of disappointments and regrets, blaming God for it all. "If God had done all that to me, I would hate him too," I said. We then introduced her to our God, who was nothing like the god she knew.

I became a Christian in ninth grade. It was about the same time I met Bob, my best friend. We fished, skin-dived, and hunted together growing up. I shared my faith with Bob every time we were together, and each time the same thing happened: I talked and Bob listened. He never argued or disagreed, but he never made one move toward Christ. Finally, I just quit talking about it because I had told him everything I knew. After high school, I went to college out of state and Bob attended the local university.

In my sophomore year, when I came home for spring break, Bob came to see me. When he came through the door, I could tell something was wrong. We sat in the living room, and Bob began to talk. This was unusual in itself because Bob never said much. He began to share some of the disappointments he was experiencing in reaching a lifelong goal, and the troubles he was having finding a new direction. I never interrupted, other than to let him know that he had my full and undivided attention. He must have spoken for an hour.

When it was clear that Bob had said everything he wanted to say, I suggested that we go up to my room because I wanted him to read something. We went upstairs and lay across my bed as I opened the Bible to the Sermon on the Mount. Bob read the entire sermon out loud. As we read we slowly slid off the bed, until we were reading the Bible on our knees. Then I turned to the book of Romans, and he read the first six chapters. Almost nothing was said, other than a question here or there. In the middle of the sixth chapter Bob said, "I don't know why I never saw this before! It is so clear to me now. I have to go and share it with my girlfriend!"

I said, "Before you go why don't we pray and you tell the Lord that you believe what he says about all of us in Matthew and Romans, and that you believe who Jesus is and what he has done for you." Already on our knees, Bob prayed and gave his life to Christ. I have often thought that if I could just get people to read the Bible on their knees, they would *have* to believe the gospel!

The Lord moved in my best friend's heart—and not when I decided that it was time to share the gospel yet again. God moved in my best friend's heart when I shut up and I listened more than I spoke.

Discussion Questions

1. How does our traditional understanding of sharing our faith damage our witness when we do not talk about our doubts, struggles, and weakness?

2. How does listening more than you speak change how you feel about sharing your faith and the process of sharing your faith?

3. What are ways you can communicate through eye contact, body language, and appropriate questions to let people know you are listening to them?

10

Sow Widely

I always like to ask any group I'm speaking to "How many here believe they have the gift of evangelism?" What surprises me is how few people believe they have this gift. I can be talking to missionaries, pastors, seminary students, or laypeople, and less than three percent of those present will believe they have this gift. Why do so few people believe they have the gift of evangelism?

Many of us don't even want to evangelize because of the stereotypes surrounding the traditional evangelist. We don't see ourselves standing on a corner carrying a sandwich-board sign that reads "THE END IS NEAR!" We can't imagine ringing doorbells and imposing ourselves on complete strangers, or passing out tracts on a sidewalk somewhere. Others feel as if they don't have the personality of an evangelist. They're not good at sales, or they're shy, or they're not quick at coming up with a response.

Good news! You don't have to do any of those things to have the gift of evangelism because there is no one method of sharing our faith. The way you do it should be as unique as you are, and as unique as the person you are speaking with. And just as there is not one method of evangelism, there is not any particular personality type that makes one an evangelist.

Instead of believing you were not made for evangelism, believe that you are the perfect person to share your faith with many people—because your personality, your experiences, your knowledge, and the way you say things is the best way for many people to hear the gospel. Some people are attracted to the flamboyant, smiling, charismatic, and witty types, but there are more people who are put off by them. Many people are in fact drawn to the quiet, shy, soft-spoken, and unsure people. One of the reasons you were made just as you are is so that you could communicate God's truth to particular people.

We don't share our faith because we cannot bear failure, rejection, or to hear the word "No!" But this is a matter of perspective. If someone fails at something seven out of ten times, they must not be very good at what they are doing, right? We would probably suggest that they find some other line of work. But if you are a major-league baseball player and fail to get a hit seven out of ten times, there are teams that will pay you a hundred million dollars to "fail." Ty Cobb failed to get a hit 6.33 times out of ten for his entire major-league career, and yet he was the best major-league batter of all time.

What's more, in traditional evangelism we consider it a failure if we do not present the entire gospel, or if the person we are witnessing to doesn't come to faith in Christ. In a real approach to evangelism, we do not have to take the person from A to Z in a single presentation. All we're looking to do is help the person take the next step, or just go from A to B. Remember, we are discipling people to Christ and downplaying the "big decision." To follow Christ is not a one-time decision, but a daily one. It is not a decision to give him all of our lives, but to give him all that is before us at this moment.

It is helpful to see our witness as a part, even a very small part, of a long set of circumstances and events in one's life that God uses to bring a person to Christ. We are just one of many influences in a person's life that the Lord may use. In this approach we are simply sharing our faith with those Christ is leading to himself. We haven't failed if the people we're speaking to don't immediately become Christians; it is not our responsibility to open the hearts and minds of people. We can consider every encounter a success if we believe that we have followed our Lord. This also means that if we say nothing because the Lord is telling us to keep our mouth closed, we are still successful.

Maybe we don't share because we're afraid of what others will think of us. We don't want to be labeled as "one of those evangelicals." So instead, avoid the typical labels of evangelical or born again. Don't behave in a way that makes people want to put you in that box. Instead, leave people scratching their heads because you act and talk about your faith in ways that are unorthodox (while being completely orthodox); they are not really sure what you are because you avoid stereotypes. All they know is that they either like you or they don't.

We need to get over wanting people to like us! It is an objective that we will never be able to attain. I can think of no better reason for someone liking me than that they see Jesus in me. I can also think of no better reason for someone wanting nothing to do with me than realizing I am a follower of Jesus.

Another reason we may not share our faith is because when we do, we feel awkward and uncomfortable. We fumble around for words and find the whole thing embarrassing. Traditional evangelism usually follows a certain predesigned method, and this method or style may or may not fit you. It would be like trying to write with our opposite hand. Of *course* it's awkward!

Instead, share in the way that is most natural for you and for the person you are speaking to. Sometimes this will mean that all you do is listen and pray, or suggest they read something. Nonetheless, being a Christian is learning to be comfortable doing things that you're not comfortable with—like taking up a cross. That doesn't come naturally, nor do many things in the Christian life.

There are two ways of dealing with our awkwardness in evangelism; one is spiritual and the other is natural. We should make it our mission to grow in both ways.

The spiritual approach is to pray and trust the Lord to guide you to the people you should speak to, and then to give you the words that need to be heard. We have all experienced those rare moments of inspiration where we feel God is helping us explain our faith and answer questions. Why doesn't it happen more often? Maybe it's because we haven't asked him, or we simply just expect him to inspire us more often. But, do you believe that a daily prayer for our heavenly Father to speak through us would *not* be answered?

The natural way of getting over our awkwardness is practice. I play golf. There was nothing more awkward and embarrassing than watching me learn to hit a ball. I made a fool of myself and endangered those around me each time I took a swing. But I practiced and practiced. Now my swing looks pretty good—just don't watch where the ball ends up!

The more we do something, the more natural we will feel doing it and the better we will become. Do you ever wonder if you have a talent that you're not using? Maybe you have a gift for music or can paint or write, but because you never work at developing that talent the potential of these gifts go undiscovered and unused. This is equally true when it comes to sharing our faith. Most Christians don't know if they're evangelists because they haven't done it enough or worked at developing that gift to see if they have any potential.

Perhaps the real reason we don't share our faith more often is because *we don't believe the gospel.* It no longer works for us. We are ashamed of our faith because it doesn't seem to be intellectually acceptable or relevant to people today. Somehow we came to faith, but we're not sure it can work for anyone else. The people we want to come to faith don't believe it so maybe it doesn't work for anyone—including us.

The gospel has always been foolishness to the world. Nothing we do will change that, but we need God's perspective on this issue. He is calling all kinds of people to himself, from many different walks of life. In traditional evangelism we believe we are responsible for people coming to faith, and in turn we tell God who we think should be Christians. But we know that opening the heart is God's work. We should let him surprise us by bringing people into our lives that he is calling to himself. Then, we will have the joy of being instruments in his hands.

Or maybe you think evangelism just isn't any fun. Well, traditional evangelism may not be, but if you love Jesus and care about people, evangelism is a party! You spend your time caring for others and talking about the One you love.

For all the reasons above and more, evangelism has become a rare event in our lives. We do just enough evangelism to keep the guilt away. But a better approach is to let the opportunities come to us, at all times *expecting* God to bring someone into our lives. Instead of occasionally planting a seed, we sow widely. Instead of narrowing our efforts, we expand them as our Lord taught us in the parable of the sower.

Would you hire the sower in Luke 8 to work for you? He doesn't seem to have any particular skills at sowing. He's throwing the seed everywhere. But why? Because he realizes that the power of the seed to grow is not in him, but in the ground upon which he is throwing it and in the seed itself. If he throws it on the good soil, it will produce fruit. Our sower is wildly optimistic about the possibilities of finding good soil because he throws the seed everywhere. I can see him saying, "Let's throw some over there in the weeds—or how about in that pile of stones? And let's not forget the path!"

You might want to say to him, "Wait a minute, don't you know that only one out of every three seeds you plant will produce fruit? Why bother at all, if your return is so small?"

His response would be, "I'd better plant a lot more seeds, then!" In other words, if few people respond, increase the number of people you're sharing the gospel with!

In the traditional approach, evangelism is like a tiny window box in which we keep planting seed after seed, hoping that this time the seed will grow. But we don't know where the good soil is. All we know is that we have a God who has told us that he is calling men, women, and children to himself from every tribe, tongue, and nation. In traditional evangelism, you try hard with fewer and fewer people. A real approach involves generously casting the seed of the gospel among more and more people. Let God surprise you with the people he brings into your life, sometimes in the strangest of ways.

We sow widely by putting more people into our life. You may say, "I don't have time for more people!" You only don't have enough time if you're thinking of traditional friendship evangelism. A better approach is being friendly and interested in everyone you come across during the day; you'll come across dozens of people each day you naturally have interaction with. It isn't about putting more people into your life; it's about genuinely *seeing* more of the people that are part of your everyday routine—who are, for most of us, no more than scenery and sometimes intrusions into our daily lives.

In addition, sowing widely not only means seeing people but interacting with them. As I've been writing this chapter, I've been trying more consciously to put this principle to work. I notice that when I'm friendly and polite with people, their whole demeanor changes. At this moment I'm at an airport, and it's amazing how a few words of kindness and courtesy will brighten someone's day. You might say this isn't evangelism; I would say it's sowing a seed. Let's see if our kindness might lead to a much more serious conversation.

A student told me he practices "doughnut evangelism." Every morning he stops at the same bakery to buy doughnuts for his study group. A couple of years ago, just before Christmas, the lady who works there asked my student, "What do you do with all these doughnuts?" He said, "I'm a seminary student and I buy them for my study group to get them to come." The woman responded, "A seminary student—you must be a good person. But I know what's in store for me, and it's going to be really warm!" The student replied, "Well, actually I'm far from perfect, but that's why we celebrate Christmas." He and his wife gave the woman a Christmas card that explained the gospel. Later, the woman at the doughnut shop was so thankful for the card and a chance to meet my student's wife. This past Christmas, my student's son delivered the card. Who knows what will happen as a result.

We sow widely by intentional interaction with the people around us. That is hard in a world where personal interaction is being eliminated. I'm a person who likes to get things done. People get in my way; they slow me down. I often do everything I can to avoid interacting with people so I can get to work being a pastor. I gas up and pay outside with my credit card. I get cash from an ATM machine. I even go to the self-checkout lane to avoid slow and inefficient clerks. I zip through my to-do list so I can get to my office, close the door, and begin strategizing how I can reach my community with the gospel. I want to figure out how I can make natural contacts with non-Christians. I put together a set of programs that will take up more of my time and the time of my attenders and ensure they'll have to rush through their natural interactions to get to church programs that create artificial interactions with people.

Is anyone else seeing a problem with my strategy? Or, as they say in Philly, "Are you kidding me?"

Instead of being "efficient," do exactly the opposite. Go out of your way to interact with people. Stop paying for gas at the pump; go inside and pay. If you do this, you could have a worldwide ministry! At the gas stations and convenience stores I frequent there are Moroccans, Pakistanis, Sikhs from India, Mexicans, and Guatemalans, just to name a few cultural backgrounds. I don't have to go halfway around the world to have an international ministry—all I have to do is walk inside to pay for my gas.

When I notice that the name on the clerk's coat is "Momo," short for Mohammed, I greet him. "Mohammed!"

He looks anxious. "Yes, can I help you?" he asks.

I say I need twenty dollars on pump five. "Hope that will get me home!"

Momo asks, "Where do you live?"

I answer, "Right around the corner." Mohammed laughs. "Where are you from?" I ask him.

"I am from Persia," Mohammed mumbles. Why do they hide their names and say Persia instead of Iran? Because Americans are geographically challenged.

"Iran? Do you know I just prayed for your country and your people this morning?" I tell him. How can you tell anyone you meet that you prayed for their country and their people? You put a map of the world up on your wall, and every morning when you get up, you stand in front of the map and say, "God, bless all the countries of the earth and all the people in these countries, and particularly bless the country of anyone you choose to bring across my path today."

I continue the conversation. "Mohammed from Iran, how are you doing? Is it difficult to be in America when there is so much tension between our countries?" I ask. Do you think that anyone else has taken the time to ask about his life? The difference between most foreigners and Americans is that for the foreigner, people are not intrusions. They enjoy human interaction. In most cultures, particularly Muslim cultures, it is expected that you will ask about one's family, and prayer is always welcomed. "Mohammed, how is your family? Your father? Your mother? Your brothers and sisters?" You can go all the way to second cousins—but make sure you're not holding up the line. If Mohammed has the time, he will share a concern about his family back home. If he says a family member is not well, I tell him that I will pray for that family member.

The next time I fill up, I enter the store and shout across to Mohammed, "Mohammed, how are things in Iran? How is your father? How is your mother, your brothers, sisters, and cousins?"

"John," Mohammed says, "do you know my father is better?"

"I've been praying for him," I tell Mohammed.

"Could you also pray for my brother?"

Need money? Go inside the bank instead of to the ATM, and speak to anyone around you. Learn the names of the people at the grocery store, like my wife does. We left France in 1998. Ten years later, on a return visit, I went to the grocery store near our home and one of the cashiers asked me how my wife was doing.

While staying with a pastor in New York City, we walked the six or seven blocks to his church. During the entire walk he lamented the fact that he wasn't making enough contacts with people and that the people whom he had befriended showed no interest in the gospel. "What should I do?" he asked.

My answer: "Take a lot longer to get to work." As we passed shop after shop I asked him, "Do you know this man's name? What are the names of his children? What about this lady? What's her story and her husband's story? What about that store across the street? What are the owners' names, and what's the biggest problem they're facing?"

My friend shook his head to signify "no" or "I don't know" after each question. We stopped right there on the sidewalk and I said to him, "You don't pastor just a church; you pastor a community. Every one of these people, whether they know it or not, are your sheep. Your job is to shepherd them. Learn each of their names. Pray with them and for them. Don't walk by them without calling out to them, asking, 'How are you doing today? How's your family? How's that problem we spoke about last week?'"

You see, you don't have to be a pastor in order to draw people to Christ. You just have to be more than a friend and have the faith to sow widely.

Discussion Questions

1. How has your view of evangelism caused you to believe that you are or are not an evangelist?

2. Share stories of how your personality, background, and interests make you the perfect person to share the gospel with certain people.

3. What are creative ways that you can describe the key concepts of the Christian faith in non-traditional ways?

11

A Different Kind of Testimony

Testimonies are powerful. They are so powerful that Luke tells Paul's testimony three separate times in Acts. In our work, few things have been more compelling than the testimonies of converts from Islam. Testimonies show that God is at work in people's lives today and puts real-life experience on the Christian faith. But there are major differences between the testimonies given in traditional evangelism and the testimonies given as the result of a normal, real, *authentic* approach to evangelism.

In a traditional testimony you're often sharing a story that took place in the past—and for some of us it's the distant past. For example, my testimony begins like this:

> I was raised in a Christian home where I was taught to believe in God and the Bible, and I believed there was a God and that the Bible was true. If you had asked me if I was a Christian and had faith, I would have said "absolutely"—that is, until we moved across town when I started high school and our family began to attend a new church.

There was something different about the people in this church, particularly the young people in the church. They had a joy and happiness that I hadn't seen in other people. They didn't seem to just know about God, but *knew God* and had a relationship with him.

As I listened to what was being taught, I realized that knowledge about God was not faith in God. Knowing facts about Christ was not trusting him and having a relationship with him. I gave my life to Christ and asked him to come into my heart and live in me.

My story is now almost forty years old. I know we sing the hymn "Tell Me the Old, Old Story," but I don't think many people—young or old—are very interested in it. If the intent of our testimony is to show how God is at work today, aren't we undermining that truth with a story of God's grace that's so *old*?

Secondly, why do most testimonies—including mine above— end when we "accept Christ"? Shouldn't that be the beginning of a long and fascinating story of what Christ is doing with the life that I gave him?

Imagine yourself at a fiftieth wedding anniversary. The husband gets up and tells an endearing story about how he met his bride. He entertains us with funny stories of the wedding day. Then the wife shares her charming stories about their meeting and the wedding. Wouldn't you consider it strange if they say nothing about how much the other means to them now, after all those years together?

The past is important, but what you want to hear and what you are there to celebrate is the fifty years that this man and this woman have had together. What makes anniversaries special is when both the husband and the wife tell each other how much they still love one another, even after fifty years. Likewise, the best testimony is one that lets those of us listening know that you love Jesus now more than you ever have, because you know he loves you more than you ever realized. We speak about the present state of our relationship to Christ.

Traditional evangelism has only one testimony to tell—"how I came to Christ." Once everyone has heard it, there isn't much more to say. We had this problem in an evangelistic small group we formed. Part of each meeting was to have a believer share her testimony. When we made it through all three of the believers, we had to start over. And we told the same stories, all over again.

The traditional testimony makes it difficult for some to ever share their testimony. What about those who have grown up always believing and never had that event they can point to as the moment of conversion? Or what about those of us who have been saved many times, and aren't entirely sure which time it "took"? What testimony do we give? I personally could give three different testimonies.

I was first "saved" at the age of 13 when our family was visiting a Baptist church while on vacation. The preacher taught from Revelation and proved the end was near. Russia was going to attack Israel, and just as the Bible prophesied, Christ would return. If you were not ready for the rapture you would be lost. When the pastor asked who wanted to be ready when Christ returned, I raised my hand.

You already heard the story of how I was "saved" again when we changed churches a little later, but I was "saved" again in college when I gave all my life to Christ. I was ill for several weeks and being tested for a heart condition. It was a rare moment when I was on my back and had all kinds of time to think about the direction of my life. When the doctors tell you they want to run tests to check the condition of your heart, this tends to be a time when you reevaluate your life. A friend came by, and we spoke about how short life was and how it was all in God's hands. Then we both gave our lives again to Christ. I don't have a physical heart problem now, but through that experience my life verse became Psalm 73:25–26: "Whom have I in heaven but you? And there is nothing on earth that I desire besides you. My flesh and my heart may fail, but God is the strength of my heart and my portion forever."

In short, it isn't the moment that we speak about; it's the process. I wasn't "saved" three separate times, but what happened is that God was at work in my life from my birth and has been ordering everything in my life for his glory and my good. That process goes on even today. I can testify to the many ways the Lord continues to work in my life.

Maybe Philippians 1:6 should be the way we think of our testimonies: "And I am sure of this, that he who began a good work in you will bring it to completion at the day of Jesus Christ." It's not about how the process started; it's about how God is continuing that process. You don't have one testimony—you have hundreds of testimonies because you have a story of how God is at work throughout your life and how he continues to be, even at this moment. You can never tell the whole story in one sitting; you simply pick a part of the story to tell.

Not only do we have many episodes to share of a never-ending story, we also can speak about how Christ has worked through different identities in our lives. Jesus didn't just save me—he saved me as a father, as a son, as a neighbor, as an employee, as a friend . . . the list is endless.

In a normal, real approach to evangelism, the real question is *which* testimony do you give? You share the one that's most relevant to the person you're speaking with. If he's having a problem with his marriage, you tell him about how God has, and is, converting your understanding of marriage. If her problem is with a parent, you share how God is converting your understanding of what it means to be a son or daughter. Many times, this means sharing the most recent way the Lord has been working in that area of your life.

But let's be honest: the reason most of us only have one testimony, and why it ends on the day we raised our hands, is that we have not seen God working in a progressive way in the different identities of our lives. We have a static understanding of salvation instead of a relational understanding. We "prayed the prayer," and now that that's over, we get on with the rest of our lives. This attitude is the unintended consequence of the traditional method. We have placed our hope in one, singular past event. The problem is, it isn't even the right event. We have placed our hope in what *we* have done—when we raised our hands or walked down the aisles—when our hope should be in what *Christ* has done. That is a past event with present implications because Christ is alive and indwelling his people by the Holy Spirit.

The traditional approach to testimonies dichotomizes our life into a "before Christ" and an "after Christ" period. This can lead to testimony envy, where we wish we had a horrible past so that we could say how good God is in rescuing us from such a life. In a real approach to evangelism, the old self is not followed by the new self, but they are parallel.

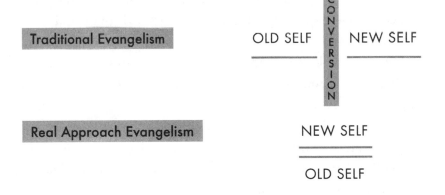

Paul said in 2 Corinthians 5:17, "If anyone is in Christ, he is a new creation. The old has passed away; behold, the new has come." But he also wrote, "Wretched man that I am! Who will deliver me from this body of death?" (Romans 7:24). Note the present tense. Very late in his life, he wrote to Timothy, "Christ Jesus came into the world to save sinners, of whom I am the foremost" (1 Timothy 1:15). Again, note the present tense. Paul didn't say, "Before I became a Christian, I was a horrible sinner." He says, "I *am* the foremost of sinners!"

This is good news for all of us who have ever had "testimony envy." We don't have to wish we had a horrible past; we have, at present if not for Christ, very ugly hearts. The closer we grow to Christ, the more we see just how rotten we are.

When I became a Christian the "second time," right away I quit swearing. God had changed me—he really had. The more I walk with him, the more I see my sin. Swearing was just one of the manifestations of a lot of ugliness that God wanted to deal with in my life, in attitudes and ways of thinking that I never knew were a problem before. It isn't that I was worse than before; there's just more of me that needed saving than I ever believed.

When we speak about our Christian experience as a distant past event—where our life is divided into a bad part and a good part—we give people the impression that *we* are good, instead of showing them how *God* is good. Getting real means you come alongside the person you're speaking with and identify with them and their problems.

I am not an alcoholic and I have never done drugs. But as a fellow sinner, I have some idea how alcoholics and drug addicts feel. I'm not an alcoholic not because I've been transformed by Christ in that area, but because I don't like alcohol. I don't like the taste and I'm not going to drink something I don't like just to feel good at some point later on. No, I am not a drunk. But I *am* a hedonist. If alcohol tasted like chocolate, I'd be a drunk.

The reason I don't do drugs is not because I'm a Christian—and it would sound pious if I *could* say it—but the truth is, I don't do drugs because I'm a coward. I don't want to go to jail and I don't like needles. Nonetheless, I know the drives for pleasures I shouldn't indulge in and the power of lust in my heart—whether it's for power, money, pride, or a host of other sins. I know that out-of-control feeling when you believe there's no power in you to stop—but thank God, Jesus has his hand on me; he calms the rage and craving inside me. I need Jesus to save me right now, more than I ever have at any other time in my life. The only reason I have not committed more horrible sin is because of cowardice and lack of opportunity, but God's grace, and knowing that he loves me even when I fail, makes repentance, faith, and obedience possible. Isn't *that* the kind of testimony we should want to communicate to others?

In a real testimony, you make it clear that your life right now would be a mess if it wasn't for Jesus—that you would be in the exact same position as the person you are speaking to (and in some ways, still are), if it weren't for Jesus. You're not good, but Jesus is great. It is a different kind of testimony. It is not a testimony of your goodness. It is a testimony of God's grace.

Discussion Questions

1. Share what the Lord has been doing in your life this past week and how you might share that in an evangelistic encounter.

2. Pair up with someone in the group and take turns coming up with ways to share your testimony with your partner. Each partner should come up with an identity and a problem that the other should shape their testimony to (e.g. identity: father, problem: workaholic).

3. How can you be honest in sharing your failures and Christ's victories?

12

A Custom-Fit Suit

I love my sweat suit. No matter how much weight I gain or lose, it fits. My wife and daughters can wear it. It fits almost everyone.

Those who practice traditional evangelism believe that the gospel should be like my sweat suit. It should fit everyone. And in a sense this is true: Jesus Christ meets the deepest needs of every one of us. Therefore, the gospel is for everyone; one size fits all. But to truly share *your* faith is more like tailoring a custom-fit suit, designed just for the person you're addressing.

Because we still live in the wake of the Industrial Revolution, we have been taught the values of standardization, systemization, and mass production. These values are great when you're making cars because mass production makes goods available and cheap so that more people can afford them. However, we should be careful how we use these values with people. It can be dehumanizing to treat people in a mechanized fashion. Yet, we do it all the time. Worse yet, we use mass-production techniques when we share our faith, employing a one-size-fits-all approach or reducing Christ's message to four or five "laws."

For these reasons, most people cannot share the gospel *from* the Gospels. Instead, they go to Paul's letters to understand the teachings of Jesus. Jesus's teaching seems confusing. He says different things to different people, and he uses stories that we don't fully understand. If only our Lord had come up with a standard presentation that had a few points, then we all would know what the gospel is and how to share it.

But again, the gospel is not a one-size-fits-all sweat suit, but a custom-made suit. The fact that our Lord didn't give us a mass-produced gospel was not an oversight on his part. He did it because he doesn't want us to tell others about him in an impersonal and dehumanizing way.

The gospel is remarkable because it applies to everyone equally, yet must be shaped to every single individual. We saw this in chapter two, Jesus's words to the rich ruler in Luke 18, where he tells him to sell everything and follow him. We saw it again in Luke 19, when Jesus commends Zacchaeus for being willing to give away half his possessions.

The shaping of the gospel so that it directly addresses and perfectly fits the person you're speaking to is called *contextualization*. Why is this important? It is the difference between a personal handwritten letter and spam e-mail. It is the difference between going to see someone in person and sending them an electronic phone call, where you record a message and it electronically calls hundreds of people and plays your message. I'm insulted when I get those kinds of calls. I got one this week where the recording began, "Hi, I'm Pastor _____. I know you're busy . . ." I hung up. Through this automated process, he was telling me he was too busy to call me personally. Modern media can potentially reach enormous numbers of people, but it is more important that we learn from the way our Lord evangelized, face to face.

A better approach to evangelism is to make the personal visit and send the handwritten letter. Everything about these approaches tells others that both God and you care for them.

I had a conversation one afternoon with a young lady who was quick to share the struggles that she was going through. She was recently divorced and heartbroken; she was still deeply in love with her husband. I knew that she needed the gospel, and having just learned a gospel presentation, I began to share it with her. I was clear, and my presentation was flawless. I knew that because the gospel "is the power of God for salvation" (Romans 1:16), my words had to be touching her heart. I was expecting her to give her life to Christ as soon as I got to the part where I said, "Would you like to ask Christ to come into your life?"

But instead of saying, "Yes, I want Jesus!" as I expected, the woman responded, "That was the most impersonal and irrelevant thing I have ever heard." I was so excited about what I was sharing that I forgot with whom I was sharing, and I never picked up the cues she had given me. She was right. I knew she needed the gospel, but she also needed it fitted and shaped to her particular situation and circumstances. And even more so at that moment—she just needed someone to *listen*.

The gospel is a message of God's love for his people, and the way it is communicated must be consistent with its character. The way you contextualize the message not only should communicate that God cares for the person you're speaking to, but that you care as well. The only way to effectively shape the gospel to fit the individual is to listen deeply to what the person is saying to you, then take what they've told you and wrap it up in a response that was made precisely for them, and only them. This is what Jesus does in the Gospels, and it is how he wants us to share the gospel as well.

Contextualization is an art, a science, and a spiritual mystery all in one. The easy part is that you don't have to speak until you clearly see how the gospel applies to that person's needs. In traditional evangelism you are taught not to let the other person speak because they can take you off-message and keep you from getting through the entire presentation. Your goal is to get *them* to understand.

With a real approach to presenting the gospel, you want to listen as much as possible because the other person is giving you clues as to how you should shape the gospel. If communicating the gospel is like tailoring a custom-fit suit, you have to keep taking measurements until you know everything you need to know. Only then do you ask that person to try the suit on.

If it isn't clear how you are to respond, keep asking questions until the light comes on in your head and you see how you should frame the message. In traditional evangelism it is believed that we should keep talking until the light comes on in *the listener's* head, but contextualization requires *us* to do the hard work of effectively communicating the gospel specifically to that other person.

In addition, contextualization requires us to not just learn a presentation, but to learn all that we can about everything God's Word teaches us. This means we must be students of God's Word and be able to address all kinds of issues with what the Bible says about them. But don't let your lack of knowledge keep you from speaking up. Instead, use it to motivate you to study. Depth of answers will vary, but every Christian should be able to respond to any subject and shape the gospel to fit the circumstances and the person they're speaking to.

There are two aspects of contextualization: determining the real subject to address, and illustrating our response so that it continues to speak long after you've stopped talking. This is exactly what our Lord did. He dealt with people individually by answering the questions they were asking, and then illustrating his answers with things and events from everyday life, communicating it all in an appropriate way.

The first component of the process may appear easy, but it's not. Never assume that the real issue is the initial problem being posed, or that it's the argument against the gospel. You need to keep listening until you know what the real issue is. This requires more than hearing the words being spoken. You must give your complete attention to the person speaking. Body language, gestures, and expressions may be giving clues to the real issue boiling just below the surface. It is a natural ability to pick up those cues—an ability that can be developed, even though most of us consider it a gift, intuition, or one of those strange moments when God gives an insight into a person's life. It helps if we are not so "into ourselves," so that we can truly hear what others are saying.

Take, for example, Jesus with the woman at the well in John 4. He asked her to bring her husband. How did he know she had issues with men? You could say that Jesus, as the Son of God, had special knowledge that we cannot have. But any woman coming to a public well in the heat of the day alone—and most likely dressed differently than the ideal homemaker—shouts, "Here is a woman who is ostracized by the other women of the village because of her moral character." We would not have been able to tell that she'd had five husbands, but if we knew the culture and customs of that time it would have been obvious that she had been rejected by the other women and that the issue likely had something to do with men.

To shape the gospel we listen, look, and ask questions. In doing so we're also telling the other person that we care deeply about him. When we have a clear idea of what the real issue is, we shape the gospel around his question or concern. Because the gospel speaks to every area of life, it can address every person's particular situation. This is why you must learn more than a presentation; you must learn the method: Listen, listen again, pray as you listen, and speak only when the person invites you to do so, on the issue they're asking you about.

If someone is having trouble in a marriage, the gospel involves applying the lordship of Christ to one's marriage. If the problem is a relationship with a boss, then the gospel is about understanding how new life in Christ applies to our work. Whatever the immediate problem, you take the person from the symptoms of that problem to their ultimate problem—the need for a right relationship with God through Christ. You speak to how Christ would change *them* in that situation.

After you believe you understand the problem, how do you choose to respond? There is no better way to answer than taking someone to the words of our Lord and the Scriptures. Be careful that it is the appropriate time and place. Many people in public places would be very uncomfortable if you opened your Bible and began reading it. A better way, in most settings, is to summarize the Bible's teaching in your own words—or better yet, in the words of the people you're with. For example, most people don't like the word "sin"; they'll talk about a mistake, a shortcoming, a weakness, or a personal fault. Start with their description to help them understand the biblical teaching, and then build upon it until they embrace the full teaching of God's Word.

This is not compromising the gospel. Good pedagogy begins with what the person knows and builds upon it, until they gain what they need to know. People today like to talk about their problems in psychological terms so begin where they are and move them to a more complete understanding of their situation.

Traditional evangelism uses stories of Jesus and the Scriptures to clarify and apply the points you're trying to make. If you only use the illustrations in the Scriptures, they will not resonate with modern people as they did with those who lived in first-century Palestine. Shepherding and sheep are used everywhere in Scripture to illustrate spiritual truth. Many urbanites have never even seen a live sheep. You must take the point of Jesus's illustrations and communicate it with a modern illustration from the life of the people you're speaking to. As you make the truth of the gospel part of their world, they're more likely to immediately understand the truth you want to convey. More importantly, they will feel the impact of what you're saying.

We want the gospel to be more than just intellectually understood. We want it to resonate with every fiber of our being. Therefore, we contextualize the gospel so that it continues to speak to the people we have spoken to long after our conversation is over.

Let me illustrate: I was in a neighborhood in Philadelphia not long after school let out. Although most of the children had already walked home, there was still a middle-aged woman with her orange jacket, hat, and stop sign in her hand at the corner I was approaching. I said, "Hello, my name is John, and I'm the pastor of Cresheim Valley Church. How are you?"

She answered, "Hi, I'm Mary, and I'm fine, thank you."

"Mary," I asked, "could you explain to me what your job is, how you do it, and why you think it's so important?"

Mary proudly said, "I help children get home safely. When the children are walking to and from school, I stop them on the corner. Then I walk out in the middle of the street, stopping all the cars, and signal them to cross. I stay in the street until the children have safely crossed, and then I let the cars go."

I said to Mary, "Do you know your job sounds a lot like what Jesus does?"

"What do you mean?" Mary asked.

I continued, "Jesus wants to get us home safely as well, and there are many more dangers in the journey of life than there are dangers walking home."

Mary interrupted, "Yes, I do know that!"

I went on, "There are things we may not see if we did not have someone looking out for us. Jesus also steps out in front of us, making sure there is no danger for us. He risks the danger, just like you do. The only difference between what you do and what Jesus does is that Jesus doesn't just walk out into the middle of the street and tell us to cross; he tells us 'come,' and he accompanies us all the way home. He also doesn't have an orange vest! Mary, you seem to care very much about these children, and I bet you would risk your own life to save them from danger."

"Yes, I would! These children are like my own kids!" Mary interjected.

I continued to explain, "That really is the same reason Jesus went to the cross—to give his life for those he loved so much. Mary, each time you step out into the street to help children get safely home, think of Jesus and how he stepped out into danger to get you safely home. And when you tell the children to cross, would you hear Jesus asking you to come?"

Mary answered, "I never thought about Jesus that way before."

I continued, "You know, Mary, if the Bible had been written today, Psalm 23 might begin, 'The Lord is my crossing guard.' Or if Jesus were here today, he might say, 'I am the good crossing guard.'" We both laughed, and then I prayed with Mary that Jesus would help her get the children home safely, and that he would get Mary home safely too.

You take what someone does every day, all the time, and you wrap the gospel around it so that their daily life is a continual reminder of God's truth. Illustrating the truth of the gospel with things from the person's everyday life, will continually remind her of the truth you shared with her.

I was working on this chapter while my wife and I were waiting to board a plane (yes, I travel quite a bit). A young man covered with tattoos sat down next to my wife. He must have seen the sign on her forehead, "Sit here, I'm friendly!" He surely didn't see mine: "Leave me alone! Can't you see I'm writing a book on *how to love and care for people deeply*?"

With just a few words from my wife, the young man was telling us the story of his life. Once again, I quickly changed my sign to "I care!" I am a professional, after all. The young man was a tattoo artist and had just landed a job in Paris. He talked about how he got to Paris and how he got the job. We hadn't been talking long when he found out that I was a pastor. He immediately said, "I know it isn't right to tattoo the body, according to the Bible, but these tattoos are the story of my life." He explained what each one meant.

I responded, "Paul had tattoos on his body . . . well scars, exactly—scars that told his life story and proved that he belonged to Jesus. Paul wanted everything about him to tell a story: the story of who Jesus is and what he has done for him. If you belong to Jesus, you want him to write his story all over your life. When you're tattooing people, would you think about how Jesus wants to stain his image on your heart with his blood so that everyone can see it?"

People have said to me that they cannot think quickly enough to illustrate the gospel from people's everyday lives. However, you *can* learn to be better at it. You can improve these skills by practicing them until they become second nature. And you can keep listening until you *know* what to say. Listening is never a bad thing!

One exercise you can do is to take a theological concept, list some occupations, and think of a way to communicate God's truth for each. For example, *sin*. How would you illustrate sin for a plumber? What was the dirtiest, smelliest problem you ever had to deal with? Sin is uglier than that. Or a nurse? Sin does the same thing as not washing your hands; it makes a lot of other people sick. Or a lawyer? Sin is like the slamming of that jail door behind you, and you know you're not getting out.

Then change to another gospel concept. For example *forgiveness*, for a lawyer, is like hearing the prison door slam and realizing you're on the outside. For a plumber, forgiveness is like that moment when the clog releases and everything gets washed away.

And what about *grace*? For a nurse, it's when someone gives an organ so another can live. For a mother, grace is all those things she does that we never see or thank her for. For a golfer, it might be playing "best ball" and having Rory McIlroy as your partner.

You can even make this a party game the next time a group of your Christian friends come over, or as a part of a training session at your church. Have one stack of cards with theological concepts and another stack of cards with occupations. You may be thinking this sounds rather childish—but would you rather give someone something that's hard to forget because its truth is continually being reinforced, or say something deep that people may not understand? Illustrations *can* be childish—but they can also be profound. Keep practicing until your illustrations become both profound *and* simple.

A landscaper was planting a tree, so I went over to see him work. I introduced myself as a pastor and said I was interested in learning about what he was doing. I asked him to explain why he had to dig such a big hole for such a little tree. He explained the importance of giving the roots room to grow and the right kind of soil. He explained how most people, because they don't know anything about trees, never dig the hole large enough. I asked him how he could be sure the tree would live. He explained that if the tree had the right soil and the right nutrients, and you cared for the tree by pruning it on occasion and watering it when needed, the tree would thrive.

I said, "You've helped me understand the Bible in a new light. There is a psalm that talks about our life being like a tree planted in God's garden, under his care. It is the first psalm in the Bible. It seems you work alone a lot. What do you think about when you have all this time? How about thinking of your life as the tree and God as the caretaker? Each time you're caring for plants, think about your life and offering it to God to be your caretaker. You might read Psalm 1, when you get a chance."

Almost anything can be used to convey spiritual truth. Practice using things around you as illustrations—a computer, a desk, a chair, the lights, windows, rugs. The point is not to use the same illustration all the time, but to use the ones that best fit the life of the person God has brought into your life.

I was sitting next to a young mother on a plane, and we were doing the normal polite conversation. She told me she was going to a wedding and that this was the first time she had left her husband

and children alone for such a long time. She asked me what I did, and I told her I was a minister. She immediately said that she and her husband had been looking to get involved in a church, but she wasn't sure; she had doubts, and faith just didn't come easily for her.

I said, "What do you mean? You just left everything you have, as far as earthly possessions and the most precious things in life—your children with your husband! You don't have a problem with faith."

She interrupted, "Yes, but I know my husband. We've been together since high school." I shared with her that her problems with trusting Christ were likewise not a problem of believing, but a problem of *knowing*. I encouraged her to spend time getting to know Jesus so that she could learn to trust leaving all she had in his hands.

But sometimes the stories in the Bible *are* perfect for others to hear—in which case we can just *tell* them. The summer we were in Detroit, preparing to serve as missionaries in France, I met a Muslim on the street. We began to talk and I told him about how Christ bears all of our sins and pays for them by his death on the cross. The young man objected sternly, "No one can pay for your sins; you must pay for them yourself! I'll tell you a story."

He continued, "There was a father who had a son and he went into town on his father's horse, and in town was doing all kinds of shameful things. The elders in the town knew the father so they sent word to him about what his son was doing. The father told the messenger that the elders should tie his son to the horse backwards, because if his son didn't have enough sense to come home at least his horse would. The elders did as the father asked. They tied the son on his father's horse backwards and sent the horse home. When the father saw his horse coming in the distance, he picked up a stick and ran towards him, pulling his son off the horse, and beat him and beat him." I will never forget how, with such violent and vivid gestures, this angry Muslim man continually raised his hand above his head, thrusting it down as if he were the father beating the son. I couldn't help wondering if this man had actually been the son.

After a pause I said, "Jesus tells a different story: 'There was a man who had two sons. And the younger of them said to his father, "Father, give me the share of property that is coming to me . . ."'" (Luke 15:11–12). I went on to share a very different story—a story of grace and mercy extended to sons, even prodigal sons, who shame their father.

Discussion Questions

1. How has standardization, systemization, and mass production impacted how the church speaks to the world? How can you shape the gospel to the questions, interests, and needs of the people you speak to?

2. Share stories of times you shared your faith but made little sense to the person you were speaking to because you did not consider their concerns.

3. Time to play: Each person in the group take two 3 x 5 cards. Write an occupation on one and a theological concept on the other and divide them into two piles. Randomly choose an occupation and theological concept and brainstorm a few good illustrations to explain the concept to someone in that occupation.

13

Evangelism Is Apologetics

When the conversation turns from sharing the truth to defending it, traditional evangelism stops and apologetics begins. In a traditional understanding, apologetics is pre-evangelism, where you prepare the way for people to receive the gospel. Not only are there different goals in the traditional understanding of evangelism and apologetics, but there are different sources of authority on which is each is based. In evangelism the Bible is used. In apologetics, logic and philosophy are used. In traditional evangelism, we call for people to submit their lives to Christ and the teachings of Scripture. In traditional apologetics, we submit Christ and the Scriptures to the skeptic's logic.

Traditional apologetics assumes that all people are logical beings who will be open to truth, wherever it might lead them. It therefore puts God and his Word on trial. In this trial God, the judge of the entire universe, must take the stand—while mankind, the guilty party, gets to play the role of judge, jury, and executioner. Remember what happened to our Lord at *his* trial? When we play judge, God is always murdered.

None of us are neutral. We all have tampered with evidence so that it proves what we want it to prove. We do this to protect our autonomy, to

135

further our rebellion, and to keep from yielding ourselves to our Creator. Everyone "has skin in the game." All facts are reinterpreted by our worldviews and unproven presuppositions in order to support our conclusions. We begin with the assumption that we are right—or at least that God is not—and come to our conclusions after we have "objectively" considered the facts.

I teach at Westminster Theological Seminary. One of our distinctives is something called Van Tillian presuppositional apologetics. The twentieth-century theologian Cornelius Van Til rightly saw that we all construct worldviews that interpret the world around us. To do this every human system must make assumptions (unproven presuppositions) about reality and build upon those assumptions a way of life and belief. Many of these assumptions are, in fact, blind leaps of unbelief—away from what God has revealed about himself, his creation, and who we are. The result is that our worldviews replace true meaning and significance with a lie, as Paul explains in Romans 1:19–25. With this lie we have convinced ourselves that our way of seeing the world is a consistent and true interpretation of reality, providing a defective foundation for us to build our lives on. These systems work (barely) because every interpretation of reality must use God's truth, but it is mixed with our lies.

Presuppositional apologetics turns those tables. It isn't God on trial— we are. The question is not, Does the truth about God and his revelation rise to the level where it meets our system's standard? Instead, presuppositional apologetics demonstrate that there is no alternative to God's truth. God's truth must be submitted to because all our systems of thought are inconsistent, flawed, and failed. God's revealed truth is our only real alternative.

How then, does one use these insights when we share our faith with those who are skeptical? First, we want to listen well. We want to seek to understand their system and the unquestioned assumptions they're making about God, his creation, and themselves. In as loving and gentle a way as possible (an approach that presuppositional apologists aren't especially known for), you want to help them see how intellectually dishonest they're being. Their beliefs and practices are not consistent, but in blatant contradiction to one another; whereas, the truth they deny is the truth they live their daily lives on.

We demonstrate their inconsistencies first by asking questions, rather than making accusations. Remember, if someone feels attacked he'll cover up and hide. Don't expect him to say, "Thanks for exposing the lies and inconsistencies of my life and worldview!" All of us are inconsistent and hide, like roaches running for cover when the light is turned on.

After much understanding, empathy, and compassion, sometimes the most loving thing to do is to drop the bomb. Sometimes the Spirit moves you to speak truth into people's lives to unsettle them. The Spirit rips away the covering that hides their lies. They cannot sleep, eat, or concentrate. The spiritual term for this is *conviction*, and God may use your words to bring this about in the life of the person you're speaking to. That said, only use this approach if you're going to hurt *with* and *for* the people with whom you're speaking.

I compare dropping the bomb with playing Jenga. I love playing Jenga. The object of this game is to remove as many blocks as possible from the tower without the tower crashing to the ground. Conversely, the objective of presuppositional apologetics is to find the one piece or pieces that will bring the entire structure of the nonbeliever's worldview crashing to the ground.

Again, be careful and prayerful about using this method. There are those of us who just like blowing things up. However, the objective is not destruction, but transformation. If you use this approach you must do it with great care. If not, you will win the argument but forever lose the person you want to win. Remember your first day in junior high gym class when you had to take your first public shower? You came out of the shower with your towel wrapped tightly around your body, trying to figure out how you could get dressed and hold your towel in place at the same time. (Why do they make those towels so small, anyway?) Imagine that just as you're coming out of the shower, an older student rips your towel off you and throws it across the locker room. This is what presuppositional apologetics does—it leaves you naked and embarrassed before the world. So use it carefully!

I was sharing a bench with a young man at a local university when we got into a religious discussion. I explained to him that I was a follower of Jesus Christ, and he explained to me that he was a philosophical atheist. I asked him how he explained the origin of life. He quickly responded, "Evolution."

I asked, "How do you reconcile the fact that if you're a product of blind forces, then your life and actions have no real meaning or value?" He objected and began defending his position. I responded, "You say we come from meaninglessness and are headed toward meaninglessness, but today means something? But according to your own philosophy, your judgments about what is noble, beautiful, and true are irrelevant!" I pointed to a rock at our feet and went on, "Your life, according to your system, has no more value than this rock. In fact, your life is of less value because in the words of Buddha, at least the rock can say it has done no harm." The young man tried to speak, but instead paused and looked down at the rock.

After a moment, I said, "It is God who, from the dust, made you and that rock. The difference is he breathed in you his life, forming you in his image. That means that everything in our life counts. Everything has meaning, and our Creator will hold us accountable." I handed him my card and shook his hand. I told him to call me if he'd like to talk further.

Dropping the bomb takes different forms, though; again, it depends on the context. I often use the (fictional) example of a conversation with a dentist, who told me that he couldn't remember the last time he was in church and felt no need for religion. If he ever did decide that he needed religion, he added, he preferred to deal with spiritual issues privately.

I nodded my head in agreement and replied, "You know, you and I have a great deal in common. Your basic philosophy in life is the same as mine, but I apply that philosophy in other ways. I cannot tell you when the last time I went to the dentist was, but I don't feel I have any need for a dentist at this time. If I did, I also would prefer to do the work myself."

The dentist, shocked, responded, "You really do need to have regular checkups. There can be problems we could deal with now, before they become too difficult and too expensive! I see people all the time who could have avoided a lot of pain, if only they had come in and seen me earlier."

I answered, "The next time you look into someone's mouth who you know should have listened to you, but waited too long to deal with a problem they didn't think they had, would you think that perhaps you're doing the same thing spiritually?"

Apologetics is not just philosophical debate. When it comes to truth, it has much more to do with the way we live our lives. The inconsistencies show up most often in the contradictions between what we say we believe and what we do.

Jesus dropped the bomb on occasion. In his encounter with the woman at the well, he could have had a long and convincing theological discussion about the true nature of worship. Instead, he moved from theory to practice when he asked the woman, "Go, call your husband, and come here" (John 4:16). The Samaritan woman's theology and worldview on worship were broken, but where the brokenness of her system revealed itself was in her long list of failed marriages. The rich man in Luke 18 no doubt had the best theological education that money could buy, and the system he was completely committed to was iron-clad tight. He confidently answered Jesus that he had done all that was asked of him from his youth. Instead, Jesus told him to apply the two great commandments—to love God with all your heart, mind, and strength; and love your neighbor as yourself—by selling all that he had, giving it to the poor, and following him.

Once I was seated next to a businessman on a short flight. He was in a talkative mood so we chatted for awhile. He was telling me all about his job and how much traveling he had to do. "I've been doing this job for a long time and it means I'm on the road at least four days a week," he boasted. As an afterthought he said, "I do it all for my family." So I asked him about his family. He began telling me about his wife and children. He explained that he had two children by his first wife, a boy and a girl (although he couldn't recall the last time saw them), and a son with his second wife. There was little excitement in his voice about his family—or at least a lot less than he had when describing his work.

When he paused, I said, "So, you do all this for your family?"

The conversation abruptly ended. It was clear from our conversation that his job and the traveling he claimed he did for his family had exacted a high price, and that he loved his job more than he loved his family.

Certainly we don't want to be rude or hurtful, but Christ doesn't always call us to be nice and to let glaring contradiction go unchallenged. Paul challenged Peter when he acted hypocritically and would no longer eat with the Gentiles because Jews from Jerusalem had come to inspect the work (Galatians 2:11). Jesus dropped the bomb, but never to be right or to win an argument. He spoke the truth because he deeply cared about people. We must be willing to speak the truth as well, particularly if we consider the person a close friend. As Proverbs reminds us, "Well meant are the wounds a friend inflicts" (Proverbs 27:6 NRSV).

There was a church in Philadelphia we were helping by inviting those who passed in front of the church building to visit the congregation on Sundays. One afternoon I extended my hand to a young man walking down the street and greeted him. He responded by taking my hand and returning the greeting.

"If you have a minute I would like to invite you to church here this Sunday," I said.

Smiling, the young man said, "I haven't got time for this. Man, my grandmother is always talking to me about going to church, and I just don't have time for this!"

I answered, "Isn't it interesting that both your grandmother and a stranger on the street are talking to you about the same thing? Do you think there is someone else who would like to talk to you about the direction of your life and where you're headed?"

The young man interrupted. "I told you, I haven't got time for this!"

"Give me one more minute of your time and I'll let you go," I said quickly.

"OK, but only one minute!" The young man was wearing a big gold chain around his neck, and hanging from the chain was a gold medallion the diameter of a baseball. On that medallion was the carved image of a cobra with two red ruby eyes. The cobra was coiled, its head raised and its neck spread, ready, and poised to attack with its fangs and tongue exposed.

"You see that big chain around your neck with that big gold medallion?" I began. "And on that medallion, that snake with the ruby eyes, ready to attack?" He nodded his head proudly in agreement.

"Did you know there is a real snake with a real chain that is unbreakable, wrapped around your soul?" As I spoke he suddenly stopped, nodding. "And did you know that every time you place that gold chain around your neck, a real snake takes that chain around your soul and tightens it one notch tighter?"

After a moment, I said, "Hey, it was nice to meet you! When you get a chance, go and speak to your grandmother about these things. *And have a great day.*"

These brief encounters, hopefully, are used by our Lord to convict and cause those we share with to search out God's truth. The best way to correct someone's faulty worldview is to continually confront them with the truth. But we must do this in a way that is both loving and understanding. By taking the time to listen and to enter into their world, we give God space to work and others the space to hear God's truth without becoming defensive.

We had a gentleman in our church who showed little evidence of a living faith. He happened to be in church when we were encouraging our congregation to read through the Bible. This is the story he shared with us:

> Until very recently my faith had been a diffident, conciliatory faith. I believed in God but in an inscrutable god, very distant from my day-to-day life, my very real problems and my hopes and my joys.

I had never read the Bible but had often wanted to. Despite having majored in history in college and having slogged through more than a few tedious and obscure assignments, I found the Bible too daunting: too many books; too many authors; too many alien names and places.

Nonetheless, I decided to give it another shot. After a few weeks of daily reading, the Bible came alive for me and I began to see how the Lord works throughout history: how history is actually His Story.

I have found the best way to practice apologetics is by getting people to listen to God's word and read his word. But we must do this in a way that is both loving and understanding. By taking the time to listen and enter into their world, we give God space to work and others the space to hear him.

Discussion Questions

1. What are the most common objections to faith in Christ that you confront? What unspoken presuppositions underlie these objections?

2. How can our style of disagreeing and presenting our position detract from our message or affirm it?

3. This chapter suggests that the real failure of our "belief system" shows up in our failed relationships. How can you turn a philosophical, impersonal discussion about truth back to the personal issue of how one's "truth" is working in their life?

14

Pray with Your Eyes Open

Christians always lie. We don't mean to, but we do. You've done it too. A friend shares a problem with us, and we say, "I'll pray for you." But being the busy people that we are, we forget. The next time we see our friend and he reminds us of the important event that we said we would pray for—the one we forgot all about—we piously lie, "I've been praying about that." And then we quickly pray quietly, "Lord, please forgive my lie and please help my friend." Or we rationalize our lie with good theology: since the Lord knows what we ask before we even say a word, that should cover my prayers. It doesn't help our guilt when our friend tells us, "I *knew* I could count on you to pray for me."

We should never wait to pray. People in trouble always appreciate prayer, even atheists. If people know I'm a pastor, they expect me to pray and always thank me for my prayers. You do not have to be a pastor for people to call on you for prayer; you just need to be known as a person who prays. What could be more important than praying for others? We are most like Jesus when we're praying for others, because Jesus is always making intercession for *us* (Hebrews 7:25).

Traditional evangelism teaches that prayer is indispensable. And it's true: evangelism without prayer is powerless. Therefore, you're taught to pray before you witness and pray after you witness—and I couldn't agree more! However, it is not only important to pray before and after you witness, but also to pray *with* non-Christians. This, too, is a way of witnessing to them.

We pray for our unconverted friends, we ask others to pray for them, but why don't we ever pray *with* our unconverted friends? Prayer is calling on God to act, and we ought to use it during every opportunity we get in speaking with non-Christians. When you pray with a nonbeliever, you're inviting God into the conversation. You're no longer talking about God, but talking *with* God. What could be more powerful?

Nonbelievers have a wrong view of prayer. They think that you have to be a special person, a priest or minister to pray; or they think that you have to use special words that sound as if they come from the King James Bible. Because you're discipling non-Christians to Christ, teach them to pray—by praying with them and for them.

When you listen more than you speak, you will have many concerns to pray for because people will share all kinds of issues. There are problems that don't seem to have a solution. There will be heartbreak and hurt. There will be questions of guidance. Each one of these is an opportunity to teach by modeling how you speak to God in prayer.

When people share hard and difficult things with me, I pray. I'm just not smart enough to know what advice or guidance to give them, but I know who is, so I take them to my Lord. What if I give them the wrong advice and they follow it, and it's a disaster? Or worse, what if I give them right advice and they think I'm a sage? I don't want them looking to me; I want them looking to the Lord. I don't want them thinking they have to come to me for answers. I want them to learn how to go directly to the Lord themselves. Why do we think so much of ourselves that we think our advice is better than God's, which is found in prayer?

What a first lesson in discipleship—learning how to pray! There are people who have known Jesus for years who don't pray. Why not show people how natural prayer is and how to make it a part of everyday life by modeling it with and for them? Show non-Christians that talking to God is as easy as talking to you. In fact, it is easier because God *really* listens.

When you pray with nonbelievers, pray short prayers that use no special words and are what I call one-breath prayers. In other words, when you need to take a breath, stop praying. If you have a lot to say, take a deep breath. With simple words and short prayers, you'll show others that praying is as easy and as natural as breathing.

Some may ask, "Does God hear the prayers of a nonbeliever?" If someone is praying to God, *is* she entirely a nonbeliever? Could the fact that she's praying make her a believer in some sense of the word? We can call her "an uninformed believer" or "a misinformed believer," but she is exercising faith of *some* kind. Were all the people who came to Christ for help believers? When Jesus asked one man, "Do you believe?" he responded, "I believe; help my unbelief!" (Mark 9:24). Jesus heard people's requests and answered them.

You should also pray with your eyes open. Why do we close our eyes when we pray anyway? Where in the Bible does it say to close your eyes to pray? In fact, the Psalms use phrases like "I lift up my eyes" (Psalms 121:1; 123:1, et al.) as ways of describing prayer.

I learned to pray with my eyes open while doing street evangelism. I noticed that when I asked people if I could pray for them, then I bowed my head to pray, they got uncomfortable because we were in public. They would turn away and step back from me. Here I was on a street corner with head bowed, praying, and just before I said "amen" they would turn around as if they'd been praying with me. I looked stupid and they felt stupid. (Besides, you need to keep your eyes open when you're on the streets of the City of Brotherly Love, Philadelphia!)

The last thing you want to do is embarrass someone in public. Ask people if you can pray for them, but tell them that you're going to pray with your eyes open. This way you can pray with people anywhere at any time, and those around you will think that you're just having a conversation. What's more, it is powerful to look someone in the eye while you're praying for him. It is as if you're looking into his soul.

What do you pray for when you pray for non-Christians? Whatever they *ask* you to pray for. My heavenly Father tells me to pray at any time and to ask whatever I want so I've been given *carte blanche* to pray for anyone, for anything, at any time. I always pray that God would bless the person I'm with, whether he's a believer or not. When I ask God to bless an unbeliever, it's code for, "Lord, reveal by your Spirit the moral bankruptcy of my friend. Show him his sin and save him from an eternal destiny separated from you in hell. Bring him to faith." I mean all that when I say, "Lord, bless and help my friend." Praying with another person is the best way to communicate that your heavenly Father cares more about him than he cares about himself, and that you care too.

Expect to be surprised when you ask someone, "How can I pray for you?" In the days when we were planning to start our church, I took a seminary student to lunch at a local diner. The waitress handed us our menus and asked if she could get us something to drink. The student and I both asked for water. I told our waitress, Sarah, that the young man with me was studying to be a minister and was a very good pray-er. I asked her if she had anything she'd like us to pray for because this would be a good time to ask—certainly God would hear the prayers of my friend who was studying to be a minister.

She laughed and said, "I can't think of anything right now." I told her to let us know if she thought of something while she was getting our drinks because when we blessed the food we also wanted to bless her by praying for her specific needs.

She left and returned with our waters. She placed them on the table, then looked around nervously and sat down beside me. In a voice just above a whisper, with her head down, she began, "I have been on drugs most of my adult life and have only been clean for six months. Would you pray that God would keep me clean?" Placing her arms on the table palms up, she pulled back her watchband, revealing a scar across her wrist. Sighing, she continued, "And could you ask him to make me happy?"

Be careful when you ask "How can I pray for you?" You don't know the answer. All I was doing was looking for some lunch and to have a discussion with a young man about working on a new church plant, but the Lord brought a person in desperation across our path. All I did was ask "How can we pray for you?" It's entirely likely that no one had ever asked Sarah that question before.

It's such a small thing for us to do, but it might mean the world to the one we're speaking with. We are surrounded by people every day who are in desperate situations. They don't know where to turn. They believe they can't pray because they're not good enough and God doesn't listen to them, so why bother? They may not even know anyone they can ask to pray for them.

The next week I took another student who was interested in working for us to the same diner. We arrived thirty minutes earlier than the week before. I asked our waitress if Sarah was there. Our waitress said she was working the next shift and would be in soon. I asked her to please tell Sarah to stop by and say hello when she came in.

Later, while the student and I were in conversation, Sarah came to our table. She looked uncomfortable and seemed to not want to talk. "You wanted to see me?" she asked.

"Yes, I just wanted to say hello!" A little more at ease, she asked if we had everything we needed. I responded, "We're fine." Then I went back to my conversation with my lunch guest.

In a few minutes our first waitress came over and asked if we could pay for our lunch because her shift was ending. We agreed and paid her so that she could go. Not long after our waitress left, Sarah sat at the counter immediately in front of our table with her back to us, rolling silverware in napkins. The diner wasn't busy now so I asked her, "Sarah, what did you do last weekend?"

She turned around and answered, "My boyfriend and I went to a movie. We saw *Lady in the Water*."

"Did you like it?"

"No, it wasn't very good," Sarah answered.

"Well if you didn't like it, my wife and I probably wouldn't like it either. The trailer looked interesting, but I'm glad you were able to give me your opinion," I responded.

Sarah said, "Can I ask you a question?"

I nodded, "Of course."

"Why didn't you pray for your waitress today?"

"I don't know," I answered. "I just don't do that with everyone."

"Do you mean God tells you who to pray for?" she asked.

"Well, something like that," I said.

"But the other waitress really needs your prayers!"

"Well then, let's pray for her right now—but let's pray with our eyes open. We can also pray for you!"

A couple of Sundays later I took my family to lunch at the diner, and we were served by a third waitress I hadn't seen before. I told her that it was our custom to say a prayer before we ate, to thank God for his goodness, and to pray a blessing on the one serving us. I then asked her if there was anything in particular we could pray for.

Putting her hand on her hips, she said, "Are you that minister that prays for all us waitresses? I heard about you, and you know we all need prayer." She then asked me to bless all the girls that work at the diner and to watch over their families. I had become more than a customer, more than a friend—I had become the pastor of the waitresses at that diner!

What better way to be known than as a person who prays. Yes, people will make fun of you. People mock Tim Tebow for "Tebowing" and they'll make fun of you too—but when people are in trouble they'll ask you to pray for them.

One autumn we held a concert series, and I was putting flyers in the windows of the stores near our church. As I went into each store I explained who I was and what I was doing, and then asked if I could put an announcement in the window of their business. Before I left I asked if I could pray for them and their business. I didn't get one negative response. All were thankful. One young lady, when I asked if I could pray for her, began to cry. I asked her if she wanted to talk. She simply said, "No. Just pray." So I prayed.

Nonbelievers have a lot to teach us. Don't talk, just pray. And do it with your eyes open.

Discussion Questions

1. Have you ever prayed for a non-Christian? How did it go? Was the person glad you prayed for them?

2. What are you communicating to people when you offer to pray for difficulties they might be going through in their life?

3. Should you pray with your eyes open when you are praying for non-Christians? Why or why not?

15

Raise Curiosity

We had invited a Moroccan girl and her boyfriend over for dinner at our house. They had been coming to our meetings and showing interest in Christianity. Her boyfriend was a Catholic young man from Lebanon. As we spoke about Christianity the young man, Joseph, said, "No one can know what is going to happen to themselves when they die."

I replied, "Yes, the Bible tells you clearly what will happen to you when you die."

With more emotion the young man said, "No, my uncle is a priest, and if anyone knows what would happen to people when they die, he would!"

I calmly said, "There are passages in the Gospel of John that are so clear that anyone reading them would know what is going to happen to themselves when they die."

"Show me the verses!" Joseph said.

I replied, "I don't want to show you the verses because I don't want to prejudice your reading of these verses. But they are so clear that anyone can find them if they take the time to read John's Gospel."

"Show me the verses!" Joseph repeated.

"No," I replied, "You may not be really interested, and if you are not, I am wasting my time talking to you. I gave you a Bible. Read it for yourself."

During dessert, Joseph asked again, "Will you show me the verses?"

"No," was all I said.

While we were driving them home Joseph asked yet again if I would show him the verses. I told him, "I will come by to see you on Wednesday. If you read the Gospel of John we will talk about the verses you find, but you need to find these verses by yourself."

The next Wednesday I went to see Joseph. I knocked on his door, and he shouted for me to come in. When he saw it was me, Joseph jumped off his bed and said, "I found those verses you told me about that promised eternal life."

"What do you think?" I asked.

"They're too good to be true!" he replied. We spent the next hour talking about *why* the gospel is too good to be true, and then Joseph gave his life to Christ.

In traditional evangelism, you would never pass up an opportunity to share the gospel when someone asked you to. You would open the Bible and go through every single verse in John that spoke about heaven—long after the person's interest in knowing had passed. In a real approach to evangelism, you stop talking long before that point.

Don't dampen curiosity, raise it. Never say more than people want to hear. If someone isn't listening to you, stop speaking and say, "You seem to have other things on your mind so I'll stop right here. Thank you for your time." Every time I've done that people say, "No, no, I am interested. Go on." But I never do, and you shouldn't either. It is better to leave people wishing you'd said more than to have them wish you'd already left.

Raising curiosity also means not saying what people expect you to say. So much of our communication of the gospel is cliché. We think we're being faithful to the gospel because we tell the old, old story in the same old, old way. People stop listening to us, believing, "I've heard all this before." And they might just be right.

On the streets of Philadelphia I was speaking to a young man who was a head taller than I and twice as wide. I had just started a gospel presentation when I noticed that he wasn't at all interested. So I told him, "You look like you've got other things on your mind so I'm just going to stop right here. But before I let you go, how can I pray for you?"

The young man said in a broken voice, "I'm coming from my brother's funeral. He was shot the other day. Pray that I will never meet the guy who shot him because if I do, I'm going to kill him and then I'll be going to jail."

I said, "I'm not going to pray for that."

"Why not?" he said with a bit of anger.

"Because that is not the God I believe in. Nor is that the hope of Jesus's message to give us his Spirit so that we can be changed. I'm going to pray that you'll know Jesus and the forgiveness of God so powerfully in your own life that you'll be able to forgive this man who killed your brother—that Jesus would so possess your life that you'll be able to say from your heart, 'Father, forgive him because he had no idea what he was doing.' I'm going to pray that the hatred in your heart that is eating you up will become love for this man who killed your brother so that you will love your brother's murderer. *That* is what I'm going to pray for. That is the kind of God I believe in, and that is the power we have through Christ!"

We prayed with our eyes open and with my hand on his shoulder. He began to weep as I said "amen." The young man took me in his arms, gave me a big hug, and thanked me for my prayer.

We were having lunch with a couple after church one Sunday. We sat in our favorite Mexican restaurant, involved in a lively conversation when I noticed the woman at the next table listening in. She was eating alone. She interrupted our discussion and gave her opinion on the topic we were discussing, taking over our conversation. She told us that she had been down to the Philadelphia protest and suggested we go down to support the protesters. I told her that I could not support the protesters because they weren't calling for deep enough change in our society.

She said, "I know what you mean. I have left the Democratic Party and joined the Socialist Party because we need real change in our country!"

I told her, "I can't even support the Socialist Party. We need even deeper change!" The woman never asked me what I meant, but that's OK. If people are not curious, don't tell them.

Another example occurred one Ash Wednesday. I was sitting with a friend having lunch when a young man sat down at the table with us, believing that we were part of his group at a retreat center. After introducing ourselves I said, "I see that you've attended Ash Wednesday service." (The ashes on the gentleman's forehead were the telling sign.)

"Yes," he replied. "It was a great service!"

"So what are you giving up for Lent?" I asked.

"Sugar!" he exclaimed. "I'm giving up sugar for Lent. After all, I could stand to lose a few pounds, and sugar really isn't all that good for you." He then asked me, "What are you giving up for Lent?"

I thought for a moment, then answered, "You know, I think that this year I'm going to give up trusting in my own works, and trust completely in the work of Christ for me."

The young man looked puzzled, "What do you mean?"

"Well, the more I meditate on Christ's sufferings and death, the more I realize that what he has done dwarfs anything I could do for him," I replied. "In fact, I think I'm going to give up trusting in myself for the entire year!" I then asked my friend to share his testimony about how he relies on Christ's instead of his own work. The young man seemed to hang on every word.

Afterward, we asked him if we could pray for him. He said, "Please! Please, pray that I would give up relying on myself and instead rely on what Christ has done."

Again, as you share the message of the gospel—and the changes in worldview it implies—never say more than what people want to hear. Don't dampen people's curiosity. Instead, raise it until they're ready to hear the full message of the gospel.

Discussion Questions

1. How do Christians explain their faith in ways that non-Christians have heard so often they stop listening?

2. How did Jesus raise curiosity when he encountered people, and what can we learn from what he did? How might you speak about these same issues from Question 1 in different ways that would raise curiosity?

3. Should you share the gospel if the person you are speaking with is not curious about it?

16

Asking Others for Help

Christians are always taught to serve others, particularly non-Christians because we hope that through our service we can show them how wonderful Christ is. Therefore, we never let our non-Christian friends serve us, but we are always serving them, in the belief that our example will bring them to Christ.

Unfortunately, this is not the case. When we're constantly helping someone, we rob that person of their dignity. They're not learning that they have something to offer others. Jesus honored the Samaritan woman when he asked her for a drink of water. If it is better to give than to receive, as our Lord said (Acts 20:35), why are we robbing those we want to come to faith of the opportunity to be blessed and to be a blessing by giving to us? We may be driving them away from us because we never let them reciprocate our generosity by gratefully and willingly receiving from them.

I know firsthand how demeaning it is to have a friend who never lets you serve him, but who is always more than ready to serve you. I have a friend I've known for nearly fifty years, and during those fifty years that we've been friends, he has helped me in more ways than I can remember. In fact, if I were to call him right now and tell him I needed his help, he would drop everything and travel whatever distance necessary to help me.

The problem is that in all these years I have never been able to do *anything* for him because he won't let me. He has never called me and asked for any help, at any time whatsoever! He will not let me help him at all with anything that he has to do, nor will he let anyone else help him. My friend believes he's being an exemplary Christian, serving others as Christ served, and he is one of the most deeply spiritual people I know. However, he has robbed me of being in an equal relationship with him. He has always made me the receiver and never allowed me to be the giver. He has taken away my dignity because I am not able to reciprocate. I would love to get together with my friend more often, but whenever we do I just feel more indebted to him.

It is better to ask others to help you because when you ask others for help you are valuing them as people. You are communicating that they have something to give, and it reminds us that we are all people in need. Everyone, regardless of their situation, has something to offer.

A study of the homeless showed that many homeless people will not go to shelters because shelters rob them of their dignity. Too often those of us in the church, who try to serve others, unintentionally do the same thing. We push people away by robbing them of being able to give to us. If you're constantly doing things for your non-Christian friend, when are they to learn that they are to start giving? However, if you're discipling them to Christ, one of the early lessons they need to learn is to serve others. Could this be the reason many Christians are so slow to help—because during their entire discipleship they have been served but never called upon to serve?

By doing things for seekers who come to your church, but not asking them to give, you encourage them to be self-serving. Conversely, too many Christians believe that they have to keep serving people to keep those people coming. No wonder we are so tired in the church. For every eight people riding, we have two pulling. Wouldn't it be better to have fewer people in church because you're asking everyone to serve—rather than to have a lot of people who do nothing?

You may object and say Christ wouldn't do that! You're right—in fact, he asks a lot *more* of us! He asks those who follow him to deny themselves, take up their crosses, and follow him (Matthew 16:24). We do just the opposite. Instead of asking people to be disciples and to learn to serve others, we pour ourselves out for them and try to make their life comfortable enough that they'll like being Christians.

Our churches are full of needy people who seem to never get what they need and are constantly complaining that the others are not Christian enough in serving them. And yet Paul says, "Each will have to bear his own load" (Galatians 6:5). This verse is found shortly after Paul says, "Bear one another's burdens, and so fulfill the law of Christ" (Galatians 6:2). We cannot bear one another's burdens until we are carrying our own loads. Therefore, we need to help others learn to live in such a way that they can care for their own needs. We should help them order their lives so that they're not in constant need of others to supplement their income in order to pay their bills but enable them to organize their finances so that they have money to give to others. If we are not discipling people to Christ this way, when will they learn it?

American missionaries suffer from the guilt of having much and working with people who have little. In the past, missionaries were slow to teach the poor people they worked with to tithe. Instead of creating healthy churches that could support a pastor, maintain its programs, and reproduce itself, missionaries—because of their "sympathy"—did all these things for the church. What they left behind were not healthy churches, but dependent people.

When we served as missionaries in France, there was a couple who were by themselves in a large city. They were good-hearted people, but discouraged because all the other missionaries were part of a team. I went to see them to encourage them in their work. After listening to them lament about being alone, not being good at the language, and having a difficult time with the culture, they asked, "What hope do we have of impacting this city with the gospel when we have so much going against us?"

"What are you talking about?" I answered. "You have all the advantages! You know our missionary in Paris. He is our best language speaker, has a lifetime of service, and is a great preacher and organizer. He cannot get anyone to help him because he does everything so well. But you, you have to ask for help. People will help you because they know you need it. When our missionary in Paris leaves, no one will be able to fill his position, and in all likelihood that ministry will end. But your ministry—if you're willing to ask others for help—will continue because you will have discipled people to do the things that you're not capable of doing."

I call this the Incompetency Principle. It requires asking others to help you and discipling them to do the things that need to be done. You need to be humble enough to ask for help and let people use their gifts. In the process, people will be discipled in ministry, and you will leave a legacy that will endure forever.

When we first started Cresheim Valley Church, we met on a major street in the Chestnut Hill area of Philadelphia. After every service we had refreshments. In the first couple weeks we were there, some street people starting coming early and asking for coffee and refreshments. We all thought this was great; we were attracting people to our church who needed the gospel. Pretty soon there were several who would show up for coffee and refreshments, but we noticed that they always left before Sunday school started. We decided that we should stop serving these men at a special time before the service. We told them there would be no refreshments before the service, only after the service. The next Sunday, half the men showed up for refreshments and coffee—after the service.

We then decided to tell the men that the refreshments were only for those who attended church and helped either clean up or set up the church. The next week only one young man showed up—but he has kept showing up. He has so many challenges; he's the kind of person you either want nothing to do with or feel you should be doing everything for. And yet he comes early to help set up and stays late to help clean up. He helps collect the offering once a month. The young man calls himself a "deacon in training." All that we could do for him would not mean as much to him as what he does for us.

If we believe it is more blessed to give than receive, we should let others have the opportunity to receive blessings. We must learn to ask others for help.

Discussion Questions

1. Why do we have a hard time asking others for help?

2. How can helping people damage your witness to them? How does asking people to help you empower and help them to feel valued?

3. Why is it important to teach non-believers that service is part of what it means to be a Christian and let them serve before they become believers?

17

Sharing with People of Other Faiths

It is exciting to be alive in the twenty-first century! Technology has made all the peoples of the earth neighbors. Muslims, Buddhists, Sikhs, and Jews are no longer people who live in faraway lands, but people with whom we interact daily. In addition, there are cults and sects—some well-known to us, such as the Jehovah's Witnesses, Mormons, and Christian Scientists, along with lesser known groups such as Scientologists, the Nation of Islam, and the Unification Church. There are also the occult groups like Wicca, voodoo, Santeria, Macumba, and various New Age movements, which are private and/or local concoctions of one's personal preferences in spirituality. These are no longer faceless and strange religions we read about, but they are practiced by our coworkers, bosses, people who work behind the counters at local convenience stores, neighbors, friends, and even family.

All these different people, believing different things, can cause us to react in one of two extremes—fear or indifference. There may be those who believe that people of other faiths will contaminate and weaken their own faith. But I have found just the opposite to be true. People of other faiths help me to more clearly articulate my own faith and have a deeper appreciation for the gospel.

Others, influenced by the "everyone has their own truth" way of thinking, don't even try to share Christ with people from different religions. What they may overlook is that there are people of other faiths who are not happy in their religious traditions and are looking for the freedom that comes from the gospel.

We were at a party in France when a woman asked me what kind of work I did. I told her I was a pastor and I was working with North African immigrants. "Do you try and convert them?" she asked. "Because I don't believe you should be converting people!"

I responded, "I don't believe I can convert anyone. But I do know that there are many Muslim men and women who no longer want to be Muslims and are interested in learning about Christianity. What I am for is freedom and self-determination. If a Christian wants to become a Muslim, they can. If a Muslim wants to become a Christian they should have the right to do so. I teach anyone who wants to know what it means to be a Christian. It is up to them to decide whether or not they want to become a Christian. I am for freedom. I don't want any person to be stuck in a religion that they want nothing to do with, simply because they were born into it."

Engagement is what Christ calls us to, not fear or indifference. We should engage people of other faiths with the gospel, in the hope and expectation that God changes lives. After all, the first century was as diverse religiously, if not more so, than the world we live in. In the book of Acts we find the gospel challenging Judaism, confronting idol worship, dealing with the occult, and answering the questions of the philosophers of the day. Not only did Christianity engage these religions and philosophies, it proved itself far superior to each of them and changed the world. We should have the same confidence in the gospel and expect the same kinds of results in the twenty-first century.

Most of us don't speak to people of other faiths because we don't know what to say to them. We don't know what they believe so we're afraid we won't be able to answer their questions. Perhaps you have a friend of another faith, and you've been saying to yourself that you're going to learn about her faith so that you can talk with her intelligently. The problem is that you've never gotten around to it.

A better way is not to read the book, but ask your friend to explain her religion, why she believes it, and what it does for her. Tell her that you've always been interested in understanding what her religion teaches and want to compare it with Christian teaching. This is better than reading a book because people who say they're from a particular faith may neither know nor believe the teachings of their own faith. There are many people whose faith is a cultural commitment rather than a religious one.

Where I live in Philadelphia, there are many Irish Catholics. They are proud of their heritage—particularly on St. Patrick's Day—but few attend church, believe, or hold to the teachings of the Catholic Church. Some even despise the Catholic Church. Therefore, studying Catholicism will not help you explain the gospel to them.

This is equally true of those people of other faiths. When we worked with Muslims in France, I was shocked at how few Muslims understood the basic tenets of Islam. They were Muslims because their parents were, or because they were born in a Muslim country. A young lady who became a Christian shared with me that she believed she would always be Muslim because she was born in a Muslim country. Culturally she was a Muslim, but her religious commitments were secular. If you approached her as a Muslim she wasn't interested in talking to you. However, if you approached her as a person first, she was interested in talking about the meaning and purpose of life.

By having your friends tell you what they believe, you'll find out what their real religious commitments are. It's good to read about someone's religion, but it's better if you let them tell you about it. That way you're not trying to tell them what they're supposed to believe.

People are committed to religion for all kinds of reasons. Don't assume that because someone identifies themselves as being part of a particular religion they believe, or even know, what their own religion teaches.

Recently we had two Muslims living in our home at different times, each one for several months. One was a young man from Afghanistan. He was very open-minded in his beliefs and would have a glass of wine with us at dinner. He did not pray or keep the fast of Ramadan. He was open to Western ways of acting and thinking. The other young man was an imam from Saudi Arabia. He was very conservative in his conduct and his beliefs. When he moved in, he asked us not to serve alcohol at dinner because he could not even sit at a table where alcohol was present. He would not touch or shake the hand of a woman, regardless of her age. He was completely committed to the Islamic religious system, in both its doctrines and way of life.

We had both of them to dinner one evening, and it was clear that neither thought much of the other. We had many conversations about religion with both of them while they lived with us, but they were very different conversations. About the only thing these two young men had in common was that they both considered my wife and me to be part of their family, and even called my wife "mother."

Too often, Christians set up us-versus-them confrontations. When this happens, both sides dig in and there is little room for movement on either side. To speak to people of other faiths you need a different approach. The arguments and proofs against other religions sound convincing to us, but I have never convinced a Mormon that Joseph Smith never found any golden tablet, or a Muslim that Mohammad did not receive a book from heaven. Attacking someone's religion, even if they don't believe it themselves, doesn't help them convert; it just closes down the conversation.

Once I went to Speaker's Corner at Hyde Park in London with a group that used an aggressive attacking style to confront Islam. They pointed out that Mohammad was a pedophile because he married a girl nine years of age; that he was a cruel, vicious man who took revenge on his enemies mercilessly; and that he displayed nothing in his character that would qualify him as a prophet. The Muslims who stood around them were enraged with anger. They were spitting at the speaker and shouting back at him. No one changed their minds. This approach just made it impossible for either side to speak with one another.

We should not be naïve in believing that other faiths are illogical, poorly constructed systems that are easy to bring down, and that those who believe in those systems will easily embrace our insights into the flaws of their religion. The great religions of the world have had hundreds of years of great thinkers wrestling with the weakness of their own system. This makes these systems virtually invincible to external attacks. They will not listen to, or cannot see, the contradictions and weaknesses in their faith.

An us-versus-them approach with Muslims is like playing checkers with all the pieces pushed to the center of the board—there are no moves. Everyone is blocked. With Hindus and Buddhists, it's as if you're playing checkers and they're playing chess on the same board. If you tell them their rules are wrong, they'll respond, "You don't know the game!"

People are people *first*! Instead of thinking of people as different from you because of their religious beliefs, understand that they are in many ways like you. They have many of the same hopes, dreams, and fears. Instead of us-versus-them, we should see ourselves on the same side of the table, talking about how we and our friends are facing the problems and difficulties in life. Your attitude and respectful listening will set the example. Before too long they will ask you, how do you deal with those issues? This will give you the opportunity to share the hope that is the gospel.

I have witnessed to Muslim imams, Hindu priests, Buddhist priests, and Jewish rabbis. If you find yourself in that kind of situation, share the hope that is in you! But in my experience, there are more important people to talk to than those who are leaders in their faith.

Not only must our approach to people of other faiths be different, but likewise our approach to different kinds of people must be different. We have all spoken to the Jehovah's Witnesses at our door, trying to convince them that Jesus is equal in all respects with the Father. We have all debated with the Mormons about how one is justified before God, and never had any success in convincing them we are correct. I had a friend in France who spent several months meeting with Jehovah's Witnesses every week. At the end of their time together my friend wasn't ready to become a Jehovah's Witness, but neither were the Jehovah's Witnesses ready to become Christians.

Instead of dealing with the most devout, look for those who are slipping out the back door of their religion or cult. Look for those who have a spiritual hunger, but are not satisfied with what their religion offers them. How do you find these people? Not with the us-versus-them approach. You find them by being interested in them and by talking to them about spiritual things. When they know you're really listening, you'll be surprised at what they tell you.

It may be difficult for people leaving a religion or cult to talk about any religion because they may believe that all religions are the same. We must share our faith in exactly the opposite fashion than they have been used to. We must present the gospel in freedom and liberty, giving them room to express their doubts and fears. There must be no pressure to believe or to conform to "Christianity." If you pressure them, they will equate Christianity with the pressure they were under in their old religion.

There was a woman who was visited for many months by Jehovah's Witnesses. They were putting more and more pressure on her to convert. She finally asked them to stop coming. This same young lady later came to one of our Bible studies and seemed interested in the gospel. One evening I felt I should "encourage" her to give her life to Christ. She didn't that night, but she came to Christ a few months later. When I later spoke to her about her journey, she shared with me that the pressure I put on her reminded her of the Jehovah's Witnesses and that she almost quit our study completely; it took her several weeks to get over the pressure I had unknowingly put on her.

When we studied the Bible with Muslims, one of the things they appreciated most was the freedom to question, doubt, and even not believe. A young man told me, "I like studying the Bible and Christianity because of the freedom to ask questions, any questions. You are not made to feel stupid for asking questions and told that doubting is wrong. You are encouraged to think for yourself!" Our job is not to pressure, but to explain and clarify. It is God who changes the heart.

When you share with those from other religions, be prepared for a long conversation over many months. It normally took Muslims who studied the Bible with us six to eighteen months to believe in Christ. As already shared in chapter seven, it took one secular Hindu woman four years to confess faith in Christ. Don't be discouraged by the amount of time it is taking. Remember, you are already discipling the person to Christ. There are many questions to be answered, many objections to be dealt with, and much to learn. Don't get discouraged if the person you're dealing with decides to study his own religion as well. This is usually a good sign because he's probably seriously considering becoming a follower of Christ. Most converts from other religions pass through this stage at one time or another.

There is also a two-step process in conversion from another religion. The first is believing what Christianity teaches. This may take place fairly soon in the process. At least they may reach a point where they don't doubt the truth of Christianity. For most people, the most difficult step is not believing but converting—changing their identity and community. Remember, they usually are not just leaving a set of beliefs, but leaving family and the way they have always viewed themselves. For many people Christianity may be more appealing than their own religion, but they cannot even consider changing because they belong to another faith community.

Therefore, people of other religions not only need to be told about Christianity—they need to experience it. They need to find a new family in which they feel completely at home. Instead of talking to them individually about the Christian faith, let them experience what grace is like in community.

A Muslim convert to Christianity shared with me that she wanted to know God. She felt as if her Muslim way of praying wasn't helping her get any closer to God, but actually left her feeling further away. She had to recite the words of the Qur'an five times a day, each time with the same words and motions, when she wanted to speak to God in her own words. The more she prayed the less human she felt, and the more mechanical it became. What impressed her most was when she attended a Christian meeting and heard Christians praying and singing from their hearts, in their own words. She saw the openness she wanted in her own relationship with God. She didn't just hear about Christianity; she experienced it.

We must not communicate that becoming a Christian means leaving behind a person's culture and all the things she loves about it, although this is often the consequence of conversion. What we need to help people understand is that Christ embraces them in their culture; he loves their foods, their holidays, and their customs. They will learn these things when we wrap Christianity up in their culture's sights, smells, sounds, and tastes. When we are interested in learning from them about their foods and their customs, we show them that becoming a Christian doesn't mean leaving their own culture.

It is important, whenever possible, to introduce people of other faiths to Christian converts from their same background. When I began introducing Muslims who were considering the gospel to Muslims who had converted to Christianity, there were more conversions. I call this approach indirect evangelism; it helps both the Christian grow in his ability to share his faith, and it helps the seeker realize that it is possible for someone from his background to become a believer. Its effectiveness lies in the fact that the person you're speaking to may not believe that you can really understand what they are going through, and that you will not be able to help him with some of the questions he has. When he meets someone from the same background, a bond is formed; he has a living example to help him.

An even more effective approach is to start a group with people who have left the same religion or cult to become Christians. If you want to reach Jehovah's Witnesses, start a group for Christians who are ex-Jehovah's Witnesses. If you want to reach Muslims, start a group for ex-Muslims who are now believers. Seekers will understand they have a family where they can belong.

Dreams are one of the most common reasons Muslims convert to Christianity. When Muslims have dreams about Jesus, they start looking for someone to tell them about him. There are people from all kinds of faiths and backgrounds who are reading the Bible in secret. And there are people praying to God, asking him to send someone to them who can help them answer the questions they're asking. These are the people you should ask the Lord to bring across your path.

When you spend time with people of other religions and cultures, your life will be enriched and your faith will be deepened, as you see God work in and change their lives.

Or sometimes, you just invite them to church.

Saidah is one of the happiest people I have ever met. No matter how you're feeling, her smile would make you feel better. One would never know the burdens that she has carried. Her big brown eyes shine from her rounded face through her long, brown hair. She dresses modestly, in Western-style clothes.

Saidah came to France when she was eleven years old. Her father had come to France thirty years earlier; like many North African men, he had an official wife in North Africa and an unofficial wife in France. Saidah was shocked by her father's actions and wondered why her mother put up with a husband who was home only two nights a week. It affected her attitude toward God. She shared:

When I was little and I did something bad, my mom would tell me that God would punish me. If I was good, then I would go to paradise. I wanted to believe in God, but with what my father was doing, I thought that if God allowed this then I did not want Him.

It was hard for me in my teenage years. I rebelled against men and the notion presented of men and women in the Qur'an. I did not like the idea of a woman being submissive and the man in charge. My family is very strict. A girl could not do certain things. I respected the rules at home but there were certain things that were difficult to live with. If we went out we had to come home at a certain hour and we were asked where we had been. I saw the difference between the way that my stepbrothers and sisters were treated and I thought it was unfair. I wondered why they were allowed to do certain things and we were not. I did not understand.

My father put me in elementary school but I was too old. I actually did schoolwork outside of school and would teach myself. I was interested in everything having to do with psychology, philosophy, spiritual things and even the Jehovah's Witnesses. They had given me a tract when they came to my door and I liked the pictures. I had always liked beautiful things that had to do with heaven but I did not believe in it.

I looked for God everywhere. I went to see a medium. I saw a few *marabous* (shamans). I was desperate; I was willing to believe anything, anything that would help me. I believed in religion. I was an Algerian Muslim. One must stay Muslim. Those who were not Muslims were considered pagans. I would pray and ask God, "If you really exist then show yourself to me, I need to see something." I was thirsty for God. I had so many problems in my soul and in my heart. I was not doing well physically or morally. I saw others around me growing up normally but I would sit often and watch movies and eat, or I would shut myself in my room, and read and write out everything I would feel. I felt so empty.

I met a North African friend who said she was going to a church. I asked her what a church was. She gave me the address and invited me to meet her there. When I arrived, I hesitated to enter. I came to the front door and wanted to leave but my friend finally got me to go in with her. I went in and sat at the back. The pastor was speaking.

I felt good. I felt at ease, yet I was very shy and I did not like people staring at me. I'm Arab and there I was, going into a French group. I was apprehensive, but everybody said hello, and they all smiled. I was apprehensive in going toward them but there was singing, and the pastor talked. I don't remember what the message was, but I was drinking it in. I really enjoyed it. At the end when he asked who wanted to give their heart to the Lord, I did not hesitate for a second—even though I did not understand.

In a way, I did understand, but I didn't realize the implications of what I was doing. I just knew that a great load had come off, and I felt really good.

Saidah has not had an easy life since coming to Christ, but she continues to follow Jesus. People may have different faiths, but as fellow human beings we are still more alike than we are different. If we listen long enough, the Lord will show us how to share our hope in Christ. And in the meantime, we can love them as Jesus would.

Discussion Questions

1. What are your fears about sharing your faith with people from a different religion?

2. Since the best way to learn about another's religion is to ask them to explain it to you, what are some questions you can ask that will help you understand their beliefs? What are things you should avoid when asking others about their faith?

3. How can we use our common human issues to build common ground with people of other faiths?

Conclusion

The Gospel:
Too Good to Be True

I shared a story in the beginning of chapter fifteen about Joseph, a young college student. I had challenged him to read the Gospel of John and had agreed to meet again in a couple of days to discuss it. Now I'd like to share the rest of that story.

When I walked into Joseph's dorm room, he jumped off his bed saying, "I read the Gospel of John like you suggested, and I found those verses you were talking about that promised eternal life." I asked, "So what do you think?" Shaking his head, he replied, "They're too good to be true!"

Joseph had been raised in a tradition where one's relationship with God was based on one's performance for God. Joseph knew that he had not done what God had asked of him; he hadn't even tried. Therefore, he was filled with fear because one day he would have to meet God. Not only was Joseph afraid of God—his life was also filled with guilt. Fear and guilt were the chief motivations in Joseph's life; however, these did not produce love for God, just a smoldering resentment.

Could it be that people reject the gospel *because* it is too good to be true?

This is not just a problem that non-Christians have; even Christians have difficulty believing the gospel. Our biggest struggle as Christians is not the indwelling sin that keeps popping up in our lives, filling us with guilt and fear. It is our unwillingness to believe the gospel because it is just too good to be true. We need again to see our Savior and what he has done for us, and to understand the dimensions and depth of the gospel and live out of its resources.

During the baptism of Jesus Christ there are two surprises and three signs that made Jesus's baptism both prophetic and descriptive. In them, we see both the majesty of our Savior and the glory of his salvation. Christ's baptism tells us who our Savior is and what he has done for us.

The baptism of Jesus itself is surprising. John the Baptist appears to be the one most shocked of all. Wasn't John the one who was to announce the coming of the Messiah? Why should he have been surprised? Could it be that the gospel was too good to be true for John as well?

John the Baptist was surprised for at least two reasons. First, John preached judgment. In his preaching he used two images to describe the judgment that was to come. He spoke of the axe being laid at the root of the tree and said that if it does not bear good fruit it will be cut down and burned (Matthew 3:10). He also used the image of the harvest in Matthew 3:12 when he said, "His winnowing fork is in his hand, and he will clear his threshing floor and gather his wheat into the barn, but the chaff he will burn with unquenchable fire." John's message was clear: the Lord is coming to judge, and you'd better be ready.

Jesus surprised us all—even John—because he came offering grace to even the worst of people. Because the Lord is patient, he offers grace. Judgment *is* coming—but not before grace is offered once more.

The second surprise is that John the Baptist preached what we *all* must do to prepare for the coming of the Lord. We too must prepare the way of the Lord and make straight his path (Matthew 3:3). Luke adds, echoing both Isaiah and Zechariah, "Every valley shall be filled, and every mountain and hill shall be made low, and the crooked shall become straight, and the rough places shall become level ways" (Luke 3:5). John's words suggest that we need to do all the work, but through his baptism Christ is demonstrating that *he* is doing the work that will make it possible for all flesh to see the salvation of God.

The three signs accompanying Christ's baptism are the opening of the heavens; the Spirit descending as a dove and resting on Christ; and the voice from heaven that declared, "This is my beloved Son, with whom I am well pleased" (Matthew 3:17). If God were speaking directly to Jesus we would paraphrase his words as, "I love you and I am so proud of you."

Each of these signs is a fulfillment of Old Testament prophecy. The opening of the heavens is an answer to Isaiah's prayer, "Oh that you would rend the heavens and come down" (Isaiah 64:1). Isaiah had just been lamenting the condition of God's people, "[O]ur adversaries have trampled down your sanctuary. We have become like those over whom you have never ruled, like those who are not called by your name" (Isaiah 63:18–19). The physical condition of the nation was a reflection of their spiritual health. God is no longer present. With the rending of the heavens, Jesus answers Isaiah's prayer.

The descending of the dove is a sign that Jesus is the promised one, the Messiah on whom the Spirit rests. Again, Isaiah prophesies about the servant of the Lord.

> The Spirit of the Lord God is upon me, because the Lord has anointed me to bring good news to the poor; he has sent me to bind up the brokenhearted, to proclaim liberty to the captives, and the opening of the prison to those who are bound; to proclaim the year of the Lord's favor, and the day of vengeance of our God; to comfort all who mourn. (Isaiah 61:1–2)

Soon after his baptism, Jesus reads this passage in the synagogue (Luke 4:18–19). It is prophetic in two ways. It tells that Jesus is the Messiah, and also tells us what his mission is to be.

God speaking from heaven, declaring Jesus to be his Son, also tells us that Jesus is the Son of David, the great king who will shepherd God's people. The reference is to the psalm where David, led by the Spirit, writes: "'As for me, I have set my King on Zion, my holy hill.' I will tell of the decree: The LORD said to me, 'You are my Son; today I have begotten you'" (Psalm 2:6–7).

In the Mosaic Law, evidence could only be accepted if given by two or three witnesses (Deuteronomy 19:15). In these three witnesses, we have one clear testimony that Jesus is the Christ, in whom all the promises of God find their yes (2 Corinthians 1:20). These three signs also describe the salvation that our Lord wins for us by his death. The rending of the heavens is our justification. The curtain in the temple was a visible sign of the separation of a holy God from an unholy people. It was a reminder that the gate to the garden was closed and guarded, the tree of life and fellowship with our Creator lost, and heaven barred. On the cross, when our Lord cried out and yielded up his spirit, the curtain of the temple was torn from top to bottom (Matthew 27:51).

The author of Hebrews explains that there was always hope of the restoration of the relationship between God and man because each year the high priest, through the blood sacrifice, passed behind the curtain into the Holy of Holies. But Christ, our great High Priest, entered not a copy of the holy place made by hands, but heaven itself with his own blood, once for all time, opening heaven for those who are his people (Hebrews 9).

Most of us have a truncated view of justification. We apply Christ's death for the forgiveness of our sin, but that is only half of what our Lord has won for us. Christ not only died for us, but lives for us. Every righteous act of our Lord—his acts of obedience to the Father; his loving God with all his heart, soul, and mind; Christ loving his neighbor as himself—also is ours. All the keeping of the Law, Christ has done for *us*. We are not just forgiven of our failures; we are looked upon as having done *everything* perfectly that God has ever asked of us. This is why the writer of Hebrews says we can, and *should*, enter boldly into his presence (Hebrews 10:19).

The descending of the Spirit in the form of a dove is a sign of our sanctification. When God declares us forgiven and righteous, it is not only our standing before God that is changed. God is also interested in transforming our character. The Spirit resting on Christ is not only a sign that Jesus is the promised Messiah; he is also the giver of the Spirit. In a scene that is reminiscent of creation, John tells us that Jesus breathed on them saying, "Receive the Holy Spirit" (John 20:22).

Paul contrasts Adam with Jesus in that Adam received life from God, but the last Adam (Jesus) became a life-giving spirit (1 Corinthians 15:45). As the breath that God breathed into Adam gave him that unique image of a God-bearer, the spirit that Jesus breathes on us begins the restoration of that image that was lost. The Spirit that rested on Jesus dwells in us so that what God declares us to be, we become. The voice from heaven that declared "This is my beloved son" is a sign of our adoption. Because of Christ, we become true children of God. All the rights and privileges that are Christ's are ours through him.

I tangibly experienced the benefits of adoption because I was adopted from birth, along with my three siblings. I remember when I was young, my mother would drive my sister and me to my dad's office. I would jump out of the car, run up the stairs and down the hallway, past my dad's secretary and the important people waiting, around the desk, and jump up on my dad's lap. I never once thought I needed to check with the secretary—I just went right in, and my dad was always happy to see me.

We also had a telephone number that was a direct line to my father. We knew that if we needed him we could call him at any time. In the same way, as sons and daughters of our heavenly Father we have access to him because of Jesus Christ.

One of the benefits that I had as a son—that I didn't consider a benefit—is that I never was without a job, even while most of my friends would spend half if not all summer looking. The first day school was out, I was at work. Even on long holidays I would have a job. However, when I worked, I worked differently than the other employees. The name of my dad's business was our family name—Leonard Brothers Trucking. While most people worked for the money, I worked for the honor of my father's name.

My dad grew up in difficult circumstances and had a father that wanted little to do with him, his wife, or his other children. As a child of the Depression, my father believed that the showing of emotions was considered a weakness. I don't remember my dad ever telling me that he loved me or was proud of me, but I knew he was. I could see it in his eyes, even though he could never bring himself to say it.

We have three daughters. In August 2005, our oldest daughter Kimberly was getting ready to attend college, while our second daughter Katie was going to Italy on an exchange program for six months. This would be the first time any of our daughters would be out from under my watchful eyes, and both of them would be leaving us within a few days of each other.

I was thinking about what I wanted to say to them before they left. What did I want them to remember if they found themselves in a difficult situation and with temptations that would be hard to resist? What did I want them to know if we never saw one another again? I thought I should lay down the law one more time. The truth is, I had been doing that for eighteen years. If they didn't remember it by now, they never would.

Just before each daughter left, I took her out for ice cream. It was just the two of us. I sat across the table and listened to each of my daughters talk about what they were hoping for in the year to come. I then shared with each one the plans that we had for them. The very last thing I said to each of them was "I love you and I am so proud of you."

If that isn't enough motivation for you to live for the Lord—to know that your heavenly Father loves you and is so proud of you—then no amount of fire and brimstone will make a difference.

I began this chapter by saying that our biggest problem is that we don't believe the gospel. If you hold your head down in shame or wince when you hear God say to you, "I love you and am so proud of you"—if you're thinking, *God could never be proud of me*—then you don't know the majesty of our Savior and the glory of our salvation.

The gospel *is* too good to be true. And once you believe that—truly believe that—nothing will stop you from wanting to share it.

Discussion Questions

1. What is most difficult for you to believe about the gospel?

2. What has been most valuable about the study of this book? What would you like to learn that wasn't clear in the book?

3. Can you point to any changes in attitudes and behavior as a result of studying this book?